I SPEAK LIFE

A 30-Day Journey from

Suicidal Ideation

to Victorious Living

NaKole Watson

I do not endorse nor am I responsible for any negativity or self-destructive behavior conducted by anyone who comes into possession of this book for any amount of time.

Printed in the United States of America.

ISBN-13: 978-1502843227

ISBN-10: 1502843226

Second Edition

I would like to dedicate this book to the memory of my precious grandmother, Annie Ruth Bethea Watson.

To my mother, Dava Watson, thank you for giving me life. You are incredible. Thank you for ALL that you have invested into my life. I am who I am because of your sacrifice. Thank you.

My Autumn Flower: Thank you for being the proof that God called me to do what I do. I will always appreciate you and celebrate your life! I'm so proud of you.

To the incomparable Pastor Audrey McCarter-Hedgepeth: Thank you for being the greatest Momma ♥ Pastor in the world. Thank you for being to me what no one else has ever been. Thank you for believing in me when I didn't even believe in myself. I love you. #TeamGodTeamMommaPastor

I would also like to dedicate this book to EVERYONE who has contributed to my life an ANY way. Whether you gave me your best or your worst, I appreciate you for doing so. Thank you so much. Oh. And to everyone who said that I would never make it:

I did.

Table of Contents

From Me to You

I am humbled by your choice to read this book. Thank you.

Please hear me. I know what it is to be discouraged. I know what it is to feel like there is no hope. I know what it is to not know how in the world you will endure the next day, or even the next moment. I understand what it feels like to not be able to trust. I know what it is to want to cry out for help but stop before the sound escapes your throat because you don't want to be treated like "the crazy one" or "the one who just can't get it together or keep it together". I know what it is to be misunderstood. I know what it is to carry the weight of the world on your shoulders and feel like no one even sees your knees starting to buckle. I know what it is to hear yourself screaming at the top of your lungs while sitting right beside someone in church who only hears the silence. I know what it is to wonder why God would even put you here to go through so much... I know what it is to think that if Heaven is all that people say it is, it makes more sense to try to escape this earth so that you can go and be there because there is nothing for you here.

I know what it is to allow razors to glide across your wrists until seas of blood come pouring out of you... believing that with every gush of blood, a little bit of the pain is going away... only to find that not only are you left with the pain, but now you're left with a scar to constantly remind you of the pain that won't go away. I know what it is to try to take a bottle of sleeping pills because you don't want your family and friends to have to find your suicide painted onto a horrific backdrop and you don't want them to have to clean up the mess. I know what it is to shop for guns. I know what it is to pray that you will be hit by a car, run over by a bus, or die in some sort of freak accident... the more random and sudden, the better. Trust me when I say that although I may not know YOU personally, I KNOW

1

everything I have just listed all too well. It was my life. I lived it for years.

Now that you know what I know, let me tell you who I AM. My name is Na'Kole Watson. I have been on this planet for thirty-one years. Because of the grace of God and the purpose for my life, I have survived AT LEAST twenty-two suicide attempts. You name it, I've tried it. The only thing I have never done is purchase a gun - I could never bring myself to do that. But anything listed on the common suicide methods can easily be found in one of these notches on my suicide attempt belt. I never understood why I had to go through so much. I never understood why no one seemed to "get" me. I was never really popular. I never got picked for dates or dances. I got bullied A LOT... I got picked on because of my clothes, my appearance, the list goes on. I've never really fit in. I've always stood out.

Sounds like a lot, huh? But guess what... That is what qualifies me to be able to write this to you today. There is no way that you can ever do the ministry without going through the mess. There's absolutely no way to have the testimony without going through the test. There isn't a single way around it. You MUST go through it to get to the other side. You can't be a pilot without learning to fly. Everything we experience here happens because there are lessons that God wants us to learn.

Listen: You're not a helpless case. You're not in a hopeless situation. You're in your qualification process. That's all. I know it seems like you're slowly dying inside... I know it seems like you have been in the middle of this storm forever, and that you can't even find a broken piece of your storm-tattered ship to hold on to... but trust me, if all you have is you, God, and the clothes on your back, that's all you need to get you to the shore. It's not over. I know that your circumstances may be trying to mimic the rattles of death. I know that there are those around you who may have given up on you and seemingly left you to die... but I AM here... right now... speaking life.

I speak life to you. I speak life to your dreams, your visions, and your goals. I speak life to your health. I speak life to the innermost part of your being. I speak life to your situations and circumstances. I speak life to every place within you that seems to be dying. It won't happen. Not on my watch. I speak life.

Day One:

I Just Don't Know.

"O Lord, how my enemies have increased!
Many are rising up against me. Many are saying of me,
'There is no help [no salvation] for him in God.' Selah.
But You, O Lord, are a shield for me, My glory [and my
honor], and the One who lifts my head."

Psalm 3:1-3 (Amplified Bible)

~ Today's Declaration ~

I am loved by God, and nothing can ever change that.

Life can be so overwhelming. It can often seem like EVERYTHING is rocky and shaky, and it often leaves you paralyzed and fearful that if you take another step, the ground will crumble beneath you. Sometimes, the only thing you seem to be able to do is lay across your bed, let out a huge sigh, and say, "I just don't know". It's okay. Breathe. Right now, in this moment... Breathe. It's okay that you don't know. It is not your job to be all-knowing. Your job is to trust the God who IS all-knowing.

Let's look at Psalm 3:1-3. In this passage, David was in a tough position. He was on the run from his son, Absalom. Absalom wanted David's throne, AND his life. That's a rough spot to be in. I'm pretty sure that David felt like he just didn't know what to do. I'm sure he didn't know who he could trust, who was really on his side, or how he was going to get out of the situation that he was in. I'm sure he had lots of sleepless nights thinking about the fact that his own flesh and blood was out to get him. However, he understood one thing: God was his shield. Wait. He knew something else: God was his glory and his honor. One more thing: God was the One who lifted his head.

Life can hit us hard. HARD! Life doesn't always seem to play fair, and there are times that we get back up from a fall just to have the wind knocked right back out of us again. It's rough. However, there is one thing that you must always remember. It doesn't matter how much your enemies increase. It doesn't matter how many people rise up against you. It doesn't matter how high your bills pile up. It doesn't matter who betrays you. It doesn't matter who walks away. It doesn't matter who writes you off and leaves you for dead. What matters is that God is your shield. God is intentional about protecting you and preserving your life. You may not always want God to do that, but God does it anyway, because your life is just that important. God is your glory and honor. God shines through you, even when you feel like you're surrounded by darkness. It's not about what is around you, it's about WHO is IN you. God is the lifter of your head.

Here is what David had to say later in his life: (Psalm 27:1-6, ESV)

"The Lord is my light and my salvation; whom shall I fear? The Lord is the stronghold of my life; of whom shall I be afraid? When evildoers assail me to eat up my flesh, my adversaries and foes, it is they who stumble and fall. Though an army encamp against me, my heart shall not fear; though war arise against me, yet I will be confident. One thing have I asked of the Lord, that will I seek after: that I may dwell in the house of the Lord all the days of my life, to gaze upon the beauty of the Lord and to inquire in his temple. For he will hide me in his shelter in the day of trouble; he will conceal me under the cover of his tent; he will lift me high upon a rock. And now my head shall be lifted up above my enemies all around me, and I will offer in his tent sacrifices with shouts of joy; I will sing and make melody to the Lord."

Have a great day today knowing that no matter what life throws your way, God is there, intentionally protecting you and preserving your life. Lift up your head. You can do it. God is with you. LIVE. #iSpeakLife

❊❊ *Write it Out* ❊❊

Think about one of the hardest trials you have ever had to face and overcome. What was it? How long were you in it? What was your attitude while you were in it? What was your attitude when you came out of it? How much better are you today because of it? What did you learn from it? Are you grateful that you went through and came out of it?

I Speak Life

Day Two:

I Keep Messing Up.

"Lie not in wait as a wicked man against the dwelling of the
righteous; do no violence to his home;
for the righteous falls seven times and rises again,
but the wicked stumble in times of calamity."

Proverbs 24:15-16 (ESV)

~ Today's Declaration ~

I make mistakes, but I choose to treat every mistake as a lesson and
not a reason to hate myself.

You keep messing up? ME TOO! I can't even tell you the
number of times I miss the mark throughout the day. I often say to
myself, "Girl, what are you doing? You are tripping! Goodness
gracious!" and I normally shake my head and roll my eyes at myself
shortly after. Messing up is a part of life. Now don't misunderstand
me - we should never just intentionally mess up time and time again,
but there wouldn't be a need for grace if we weren't going to make
mistakes from time to time.

Proverbs 24:16 teaches us that the children of God (yourself
included) are prone to "fall" at times. There are times when pride

gets the best of us. We mismanage our money sometimes. We get mad and say ugly things to each other sometimes. We say negative things to ourselves about ourselves sometimes. We do things that are displeasing to God sometimes. We ALL do. HOWEVER, what is amazing about when the righteous fall is that not only do they fall, but they RISE AGAIN. Anyone can fall, but it takes a special degree of empowerment to be able to get back up again.

During my thirty-one years here, I have fallen more times than I care to count. I have failed tests, bombed job interviews, lost good jobs, messed up wonderful relationships, lost homes and cars… the list goes on. I felt like a failure, and I felt like I would never be able to do anything right. I felt like I was a mistake and a waste of space on this earth. I hated the fact that I kept messing up time and time again. But do you know what I noticed after a while? I noticed that I was still standing. No matter how low I got, and no matter how many times I fell, there was a God who was right there waiting to help me to rise again.

Here's the thing, though. The Bible doesn't say that the righteous fall and God picks them up and carries them where they need to go. The Bible says that the righteous fall and that the righteous RISE again. That indicates that there is something that we must do. I'll leave you with this passage of scripture from the New Testament:

Mark 9:14-27 (ESV)

"And when they came to the disciples, they saw a great crowd around them, and scribes arguing with them. And immediately all the crowd, when they saw him, were greatly amazed and ran up to him and greeted him. And he asked them, "What are you arguing about with them?" And someone from the crowd answered him,

"Teacher, I brought my son to you, for he has a spirit that makes him mute. And whenever it seizes him, it throws him down, and he foams and grinds his teeth and becomes rigid. So I asked your disciples to cast it out, and they were not able." And he answered them, "O faithless generation, how long am I to be with you? How long am I to bear with you? Bring him to me." And they brought the boy to him. And when the spirit saw him, immediately it convulsed the boy, and he fell on the ground and rolled about, foaming at the mouth. And Jesus asked his father, "How long has this been happening to him?" And he said, "From childhood. And it has often cast him into fire and into water, to destroy him. But if you can do anything, have compassion on us and help us." And Jesus said to him, "'If you can'! All things are possible for one who believes." Immediately the father of the child cried out[d] and said, "I believe; help my unbelief!" And when Jesus saw that a crowd came running together, he rebuked the unclean spirit, saying to it, "You mute and deaf spirit, I command you, come out of him and never enter him again." And after crying out and convulsing him terribly, it came out, and the boy was like a corpse, so that most of them said, "He is dead." But Jesus took him by the hand and lifted him up, and he arose."

I know. You messed up. Badly. I know you did. It hurts… I know it hurts. You don't want to be known as a failure. You don't want to try anymore because your previous attempts have failed. You don't want to be like the boy who had the same issue since childhood. You don't want to be the person who has been carrying around the same issues year after year, always falling on the ground and letting what you're carrying run its course until it finally decides to let you go. Trust me when I tell you that I understand,

and trust me when I tell you that I have good news. Jesus rebuked the unclean spirit and told the spirit to never enter the boy again. Today, right now, I rebuke any unclean spirit that has taken residence in your life. I command that spirit to flee and to NEVER return again. EVER. Now this next part may sting, and it may be uncomfortable, but whatever is holding you HAS to let you go. It will fight coming out, but the focus isn't on the fight. The focus is on the fact that it is coming out. It is letting you go. It is leaving you alone. Fear, doubt, unforgiveness, disease (dis-ease), anxiety, suicidal ideation, whatever it is… It is leaving your life.

The process may not be instantaneous like that of this young boy in the scripture, but that doesn't mean that the process isn't happening. It may take a lot of strength out of you, and those around you may not understand what is going on… but Jesus took the boy by the hand… and lifted him up… AND HE AROSE. Isn't it amazing that it wasn't until the boy was completely depleted of HIS strength that he was given the supernatural ability to arise?

Today… Right now… I am telling you to arise. Rise and shine. This message has lifted you up… The only thing left to do now is to rise. Take your rightful place. Walk in your dominion. Walk in your authority. Stand in your power. The beautiful thing is that even if you take a few steps and fall again, the hand of God is right there to lift you up… and that same power will be right there within you to help you to arise all over again. It gets easier and easier each time once you realize that it is all making you better.

Have a wonderful day today… Keep walking… Keep rising… Higher… higher… higher. LIVE! #iSpeakLife

❖❖ *Write it Out* ❖❖

(Spiritually and/or naturally:) How does it make you feel when you see someone fall? Do you laugh? Do you become anxious? Do you try to help? How do you feel when YOU fall? Let this journal entry shine the light on how you view and respond to the falls of others vs how you would want others to view and respond to yours.

Day Three:
I Will Never Be Good Enough

"Lie not in wait as a wicked man against the dwelling of the
righteous; do no violence to his home;
for the righteous falls seven times and rises again,
but the wicked stumble in times of calamity."

Psalm 139:13-14 (ESV)

~ Today's Declaration ~

I am worth more than I will ever be able to imagine.

For who? You'll never be good enough… for who? Who is
it that you're trying to please? Who are you trying to impress? Who
are you living for?

Let me tell you a personal story. I spent the majority of my
life living for the approval of others. Even now, there are certain
people in my life that I always want to get approval from. They
used to carry so much weight in my life that if I didn't have their
approval, I didn't feel like what I was doing was worth anything. I
didn't feel like who I AM was worth anything. That's not a good
place to be in. It's so unpredictable and unstable, because it's

predicated on something that only the other individual(s) can control. We allow people to carry way too much weight in our lives. Take your power back!

As I got ready to write this book, I realized something. My purpose is not dependent upon the opinions of others. God didn't have a meeting with them before deciding to allow me to come forth in this earthly realm.

Now don't get me wrong: we need people in our lives. We need people who can and will vouch for us. We need witnesses, supporters, and all of that. However, that need doesn't outweigh the fact that with or without the approval of others, God's love for us is the same. Our value is the same.

The Bible says that YOU are fearfully and wonderfully made. Who you are is a wonderful work of God - flaws and all. God made you just the way you are, and despite what society, friends, and/or family may tell you, you ARE good enough. You ARE loved. You ARE valued. You ARE precious in the sight of God.

Never allow the opinions of others to dim your light. You were created to shine. Yes, it hurts when those you love don't seem to love you the same way. Yes, it stings when you treat others like they are good enough but they treat you like you'll never really be worthy of their love. It's painful. It seems unfair. But... None of that determines your value. Always remember that.

God formed everything about you. Every part. Every wrinkle. Every freckle. Every hair. Every dimple. ALL of you was formed by God. That makes you good enough. That trumps any effort anyone could ever make to try to bring you down. God took the time to personally craft you with hands full of love. You can't beat that.

Don't you ever again base your worth on the approval of others. They're not your Creator, so they'll never be able to truly validate you anyway. Go forward in this day knowing that you ARE good enough. Your soul already knows it... You just need to send a quick reminder to your mind. LIVE. #iSpeakLife

❖❖ *Write it Out* ❖❖

What are three things you love about yourself? Why do you love these things? Were you born with these things or did they develop over time? What do you do throughout the day to affirm your value and God's love for you? If you don't do anything, what (if anything) do you vow to start doing?

Day Four:

Lack

"The Lord is my shepherd; I shall not want. He makes me lie down in green pastures. He leads me beside still waters. He restores my soul. He leads me in paths of righteousness for his name's sake. Even though I walk through the valley of the shadow of death, I will fear no evil, for you are with me; your rod and your staff, they comfort me. You prepare a table before me in the presence of my enemies; You anoint my head with oil; my cup overflows. Surely goodness and mercy shall follow me all the days of my life, and I shall dwell in the house of the Lord forever."

Psalm 23 (ESV)

~ Today's Declaration ~

I walk in abundance, and lack is not what God desires for me.

Today's passage of scripture is a very familiar one. In this passage, David equates his relationship with God to that of a sheep and a shepherd. He speaks about God's love and concern for all of us. This concern isn't just present in the good times, but it is present in the bad times as well.

God takes care of us. Even when we don't have everything we feel that we want or need, we have to trust and believe that we are right where we need to be. If there is a need or a lack, it is either because there is something for us to learn and/or do in order to resolve the lack, or it is because God desires for us to learn to trust.

Trusting God is HARD. Very hard. I remember being homeless and going days without really knowing how I was going to eat, drink, bathe, etc. The "bare necessities" were hot commodities for me. I can remember sleeping in a cold house and burning candles because there was no electricity. I remember breaking packs of noodles in half and cooking them with the gas stove using water that I stole from the outside faucet at a store up the street. Times were HARD. I remember only having crackers and water to last me throughout the day.

Those times were very trying for me. As David put it, I felt like I was walking, more like crawling, "through the valley of the shadow of death". I remember wondering, "Where are all of the church people? Where are all the people that I have served, given to, supported, loved... where are they now?" I attempted suicide several times during this period of my life (about four months). It was rough. It was tough. It was bad. I lost A LOT. I didn't know what I was going to do. Lack had become my lifestyle.

Yet.... Even in the midst of my lack... Even in the midst of homelessness, heartache, and despair... SOMEHOW... I found peace. God was my peace. To this day, God IS my peace. God leads me beside still waters to remind me of the peace that has been given to me. God restores my soul. It's amazing. God anoints my head with oil... and my cup overflows. I KNOW for a FACT that God's goodness and mercy will definitely follow me for the rest of my life, and I know that I will be with God and rest in God FOREVER. I have no doubt about that.

My times of lack were hard. They took a lot out of me. I felt like a hypocrite because I would pray for everyone else and see results but there didn't seem to be any results in my own life. I HATED my life. I HATED myself for some of the decisions that I had made. I HATED feeling like I had been put on this earth to suffer...

But when I look back, I have such an appreciation for that time in my life. That time taught me how to appreciate the little things. I don't ask for lavish things. Honestly, I don't really ask God for material things unless I absolutely need them... I'm just not that type of person anymore. I have nice things, but most of them have been given to me. The Lord is my shepherd. I shall not want. I live by that. I wouldn't have known how to live by that if I hadn't experienced those times of lack. I mentioned one, but there have been many, many more.

You may be experiencing lack in your relationships, finances, transportation, etc. but I am here to tell you that God sees. God knows. God handles all. Trust God for what you need. Acknowledge God's place in your life, and you SHALL NOT WANT. It's law. You shall not want. Remember that. LIVE in that.

Have a great day today, and focus on what you have been given. The rest will come to you in God's perfect timing. LIVE. #iSpeakLife

✾ *Write it Out* ✾

What is something you can do today to help someone you know who is currently going through a rough time?

Na'Kole Watson

Day Five:

Why Am I Even Here?

"Though I walk in the midst of trouble, you preserve my life; you stretch out your hand against the wrath of my enemies, and your right hand delivers me. The Lord will fulfill his purpose for me; your steadfast love, O Lord, endures forever. Do not forsake the work of your hands."

Psalm 138:7-8 (ESV)

~ Today's Declaration ~

I will be everything that God has purposed for me to be.

When you go through a lot of trials back-to-back, you often wonder if there is even a purpose for you being here. Clearly God didn't put you here just to suffer... right? You wonder if maybe you missed the mark and now your life will never be what it was intended to be.

Life isn't easily understood at face value. It honestly doesn't make a lot of sense at times. If you have been dealt a lot of "bad hands" lately, you may feel like there is no point in being here at all, and that may be what has driven or what continues to drive you to feel like taking your life. I understand. I have no judgement for you about that. I have been there.

I can remember wandering aimlessly through life and just reacting to whatever came my way. I wasn't intentional about anything because I felt like I was just some random person who had randomly been put here for some random reason that I would never discover. Not knowing your purpose can be frustrating, confusing, and disheartening... but you must remember that just because you don't know something doesn't mean that God doesn't know.

I have used a lot of David's words so far in this devotional. David's life gives us such a great depiction of the trials, tribulations, feelings, and situations that we encounter every day. David kept it real, and he didn't mind being honest with his feelings.

The first verse in this passage talks about how even though we are going through troubles, God is still preserving our lives. I know it seems like torture sometimes, but remember what we discussed earlier. We are in our qualification process right now. David says that God's right hand delivers us... and we know (or now you know) that the right hand is the hand of authority. God has the authority to deliver us out of the situations we face. Isn't that good to know?

In the next verse, David lets us know something that is very important for us to remember, especially when we aren't able to clearly see the meaning behind all that we are facing. GOD will fulfill every single purpose for us. Every single one. It is God's enduring and unfailing love that serves as the glue that holds us together and keeps us grounded in the midst of what we are going through. It is that love that caused God to intentionally create YOU to be exactly who you are and to do what only you can do.

You bring your own unique spice and pizazz to this experience we call life. You are valued, and you are needed.

EVERYTHING... whether it seems good or bad... has a purpose. EVERYTHING. EVERYONE... even you. Yes, you. You may not know exactly what it is now, but the fact that you are breathing lets me know that it's there. One of the most beautiful things about this life is being able to take the journey into what God already knows: your purpose. I know it may seem hard at times, but don't give up on your journey. It's going to get better... and you're going to LIVE to testify about it. I'm pulling for you. I believe in you. I know that you're here for a reason, and I won't stop praying that you find out and totally embrace and embody what that reason is. LIVE. #iSpeakLife

✱✱ *Write it Out* ✱✱

Think of something that you have previously deemed to be insignificant (a place, a job, an animal, etc.) and rethink it. What is its purpose? Why do you think you are here?

Day Six:

They Didn't Even Apologize.

"Then Peter came up and said to him, 'Lord, how often will my brother sin against me, and I forgive him? As many as seven times?' Jesus said to him, 'I do not say to you seven times, but seventy-seven times. Therefore the kingdom of heaven may be compared to a king who wished to settle accounts with his servants. When he began to settle, one was brought to him who owed him ten thousand talents. And since he could not pay, his master ordered him to be sold, with his wife and children and all that he had, and payment to be made. So the servant fell on his knees, imploring him, 'Have patience with me, and I will pay you everything.' And out of pity for him, the master of that servant released him and forgave him the debt. But when that same servant went out, he found one of his fellow servants who owed him a hundred denarii, and seizing him, he began to choke him, saying, 'Pay what you owe.' So his fellow servant fell down and pleaded with him, 'Have patience with me, and I will pay you.' He refused and went and put him in prison until he should pay the debt. When his fellow servants saw what had taken place, they were greatly distressed, and they went and reported to their master all that had taken place. Then his master summoned him and said to him, 'You wicked servant! I forgave you all that debt because you pleaded with me. And should not you have had mercy on your fellow servant, as I had mercy on you?' And in anger his master delivered him to the jailers, until he should pay all his debt. So also my heavenly Father will do to every one of you, if you do not forgive your brother from your heart.'"

Matthew 18:21-35 (ESV)

~ Today's Declaration ~

Today I release everyone who hurt me – whether they apologized or not.

There is nothing worse than hearing someone speak or preach about pride and knowing that the person operates in pride when it comes to you. There is nothing like hearing someone talk about how we shouldn't abuse others but never acknowledging the way that they abuse (or have abused) you. There is nothing like hearing someone spell out from a-z how you are supposed to treat someone, but noticing that they never seem to know how to treat you. I know all of these things all too well, and they can all be very upsetting to deal with.

Jesus does not mince words when it comes to forgiveness. Our instructions about forgiveness are simple: FORGIVE. There aren't any stipulations or backend clauses that deal with whether or not the person apologizes, whether or not the apology is sincere, or any of that. We have to forgive. Period.

This is challenging at times, because it hurts us to know that someone could mistreat us and not even acknowledge it. Sometimes we feel like hearing the person acknowledge that they hurt us will somehow ease the pain. This may be true, but unfortunately, you won't always get to hear that apology. There are people who will (for whatever reason) treat you wrong, KNOW that they treat your wrong, and NEVER acknowledge it. Does it hurt? Yes. Does it diminish your value? No. Does it excuse you from having to forgive them? NO! Absolutely not.

Jesus tells a story of a king who wanted to "settle up" with all of his servants. There was one servant in particular who needed a little bit more time to pay. The king granted his request... and what did the servant do? He went out and found someone who owed him and instead of doing the same thing the king had done to him, he attacked the person and demanded that he pay up. The person made the exact same request that the servant had made to the king, but the servant denied the request. When the king found out about this, he put the servant in jail. Why? Because how do you come to me for mercy and then not want to show that mercy for others?

The story ends with Jesus saying that God will do the same thing to us if we do not forgive... but not just forgive - forgive FROM OUR HEARTS. That right there is a hard thing to do. I get it. Totally. It makes it even harder when the person doesn't even have the decency to acknowledge and/or apologize for what they have done. But, as you see in this passage, none of that changes the commandment. We have to forgive. Forgiveness is not about the other person. It's about US. It keeps US free. It keeps the blessings flowing our way.

The fact of the matter is that you may never get an apology. Ever in life. The person may be too prideful to apologize. The person may genuinely not believe that they were wrong. The person may not know that they upset you. Whatever the reason, none of them change the command. Your Ego (also known as "the flesh") doesn't want to do this, because of its need to feel vindicated - but I'm here to tell you and your Ego that you need to let it go. You'll feel better. It doesn't change the fact that you were mistreated. It doesn't change the fact that the person was wrong... but can I ask you something? How many people in YOUR life do YOU need to apologize to? Puts it into perspective, huh?

Today I want you to make a decision to let it go. It happened. You're still here. You have your whole life ahead of you. I'm not asking you to be a doormat. I'm not asking you to let people treat you any and every kind of way. I'm asking you to let it go... for YOUR benefit. You'll live a healthier life. You'll sleep better at night. I know they didn't apologize. I know it hurts. I know it seems unfair... but you can't live there. You have to LIVE in the freedom that forgiveness brings. You can do it. It's a matter of choice.

Have a wonderful day today, and LIVE in the freedom of being forgiving and giving forgiveness. I believe in you, and I KNOW that you can do this! #iSpeakLife

✵ *Write it Out* ✵

Is there anyone that you need to apologize to? Write out your apology here and allow God to deal with your heart about how and when to give it. Come on... You can do it!

Day Seven:

Church Folks!

"And behold, a lawyer stood up to put him to the test, saying, 'Teacher, what shall I do to inherit eternal life?' He said to him, 'What is written in the Law? How do you read it?' And he answered, 'You shall love the Lord your God with all your heart and with all your soul and with all your strength and with all your mind, and your neighbor as yourself.' And he said to him, 'You have answered correctly; do this, and you will live.' But he, desiring to justify himself, said to Jesus, 'And who is my neighbor?' Jesus replied, 'A man was going down from Jerusalem to Jericho, and he fell among robbers, who stripped him and beat him and departed, leaving him half dead. Now by chance a priest was going down that road, and when he saw him he passed by on the other side. So likewise a Levite, when he came to the place and saw him, passed by on the other side. But a Samaritan, as he journeyed, came to where he was, and when he saw him, he had compassion. He went to him and bound up his wounds, pouring on oil and wine. Then he set him on his own animal and brought him to an inn and took care of him. And the next day he took out two denarii and gave them to the innkeeper, saying, 'Take care of him, and whatever more you spend, I will repay you when I come back.' Which of these three, do you think, proved to be a neighbor to the man who fell among the robbers?' He said, 'The one who showed him mercy.' And Jesus said to him, 'You go, and do likewise.'"

Luke 10:25-37 (ESV)

~ Today's Declaration ~

I am forgiven, therefore I forgive.

This one right here... I'm sure you chuckled a little bit, shook your head, and maybe even rolled your eyes when you saw the title. Good ole church folks! I could write an entire series of books about the things that I have experienced in the church... but, believe it or not, today's devotional really isn't going in that direction.

Now that we have cleared that up, let's look at the text. There was a man who was really having a rough time. He was headed from one city to another, and some robbers came through, took his clothes, beat him down, and left him for dead. Sound familiar? I know you can relate to that feeling... Robbed of what you had.... Embarrassed... Left for dead.

To add insult to injury, a priest (church person) came by and saw this man helpless on the ground... and decided to cross the road and pass on the other side... I guess he had to hurry up and get to church. Then there was the Levite (Levites assisted with worship in the temple) ... and I guess he had somewhere to be too, because he did the exact same thing that the priest did. Next came the Samaritan. To give you a little historical context, the Samaritans weren't really popular at this time. They were like the "lames" and "rejects" of today's society (although I obviously don't think anyone is "lame" or a "reject") ... The Samaritan man came through, and instead of just turning his head and walking to the other side as if he didn't see this man wallowing around helplessly on the ground, he had compassion. He stopped what he was doing, and he helped the man. He got him all cleaned up, put ointment on his wounds, wrapped him up, and took him to an inn. He stayed there at the inn overnight to take care of him. When morning came, he told the innkeeper to continue to care for him, and he assured the innkeeper that he would pay the expense on his return trip.

So... after Jesus tells this story to the lawyer who asked Him the initial question about how to inherit eternal life, He asks the question: "Which of these three, do you think, proved to be a neighbor to the man who fell among the robbers?" The lawyer answered that it would be the one who showed mercy. Jesus said to him, "You go, and do likewise."

Listen. Jesus didn't harp on the fact that those who were supposed to be the "church folks" didn't help the man. He didn't go on a long monologue about how wrong they were and how they could have and should have done better. He simply told the lawyer to go and do what the Samaritan (the good Samaritan) did. That was it.

We have an expectation that people who regularly attend church should behave in a certain manner... and they absolutely should. However, that is not always the case. Yes, it hurts deeply when those who profess to be followers of Christ do things that are clearly against what Christ stands for. However, what you must always remember is that in your life, what matters the most is how you respond to the things that come your way. That is what God looks at. That's what God honors. Now that doesn't mean that you can't or won't get offended. It doesn't mean that you can't or won't be hurt. If anyone understands "church hurt", God knows I do. However, at the end of the day, our confidence and trust has to remain in God. We can't focus so much on "church folks" not living up to their name that we miss God. Ultimately, that's who our relationship is with anyway.

I would like to offer you a perspective change. When you go to church, don't think about the people and what they are doing and not doing. Think of it like this: God has you in whatever place for whatever season for a reason that God is very intentional about. Don't look at your situation through natural eyes. See it in the Spirit. That's the only way it will make sense. Every time someone was wounded by church folks or anyone else for that matter, there was a purpose working in the background. There is always a purpose in your pain. That doesn't mean that you stick around in an abusive situation. It doesn't mean that you allow yourself to be mishandled... It simply means that in ALL THINGS, you trust God. God didn't leave that man on the side of the road. Church folks may have, but God didn't.

Not all church people fall in the same category, so please don't ever think that every Christian is bad - I am only making the "church folks" generalization for the sake of the point of this message. There are lots of people in the church who represent Christ to the fullest and live out the teachings of Jesus every day. Strive to be one of them. LIVE to exemplify what you know will be pleasing to God. That's all you're responsible for.

Have a peaceful day today... and LIVE. It's gonna be okay. Make sure that you're about that Good Samaritan life from this day forward. Some people are brought in our lives for the specific purpose of showing us how NOT to be. Make sure that you don't turn into the very thing that you know you shouldn't be. "Church folks" have souls too. We all do. We all miss the mark. We all need improvement. Everything is working out just fine, and you will be okay. Change your perspective. Focus on your amazing future, and not on what others have done to you in the past. You're still here. LIVE. #iSpeakLife

❖❖ *Write it Out* ❖❖

Think of a time when YOU behaved like the priest and the Levite in the story. If you could relive that moment, would you do things differently? After reading today's devotional, how will you deal with disappointments you experience within the household of faith? Will they run you away, or will they drive you closer to God?

Day Eight:

Misunderstood.

"And he went up on the mountain and called to him those whom he desired, and they came to him. And he appointed twelve (whom he also named apostles) so that they might be with him and he might send them out to preach and have authority to cast out demons. He appointed the twelve: Simon (to whom he gave the name Peter); James the son of Zebedee and John the brother of James (to whom he gave the name Boanerges, that is, Sons of Thunder); Andrew, and Philip, and Bartholomew, and Matthew, and Thomas, and James the son of Alphaeus, and Thaddaeus, and Simon the Zealot, and Judas Iscariot, who betrayed him. Then he went home, and the crowd gathered again, so that they could not even eat. And when his family heard it, they went out to seize him, for they were saying, 'He is out of his mind.'"

Mark 3:13-21 (ESV)

~ Today's Declaration ~

Today, I embrace who I am. God understands.

Being misunderstood is a hard thing. Being misunderstood by those you love the most is even harder. No one wants to feel like their friends and family members have no idea who they are or no concept of what it is that they're doing. That's an awful feeling.

It's amazing how in this passage, it was those who were close to Jesus who thought and even said that He was "out of his mind". Can you imagine knowing that you were here to bridge the gap between man and God while living with the fact that the very people you were sent to help don't even understand you? That's a lot to deal with... but Jesus handled it well. He kept on doing what He was sent to do.

I cannot tell you how many YEARS of my life I have wasted trying to get people to understand me. I have exhausted all of my efforts... and they still don't understand. Is it disheartening? Very. However, I'm about to share with you a realization that changed my life.

Have you ever gone to an art gallery or seen a painting somewhere that looked like a toddler just splashed some colors on a canvas? Have you ever seen the artist who painted the painting come out and explain exactly what it is, and noticed that while he/she is explaining it, you become crystal clear on what it is? Or maybe you looked at the artist like, "Naahhh... I don't see it..."? Either way, the beautiful thing about art, is that it only has to be understood by the people that it is intended for. If a piece doesn't "catch your eye", it is safe to say that the piece wasn't intended for you.

The same thing holds true in our lives. We often forget that just because people are around us all the time doesn't mean that they are the people that our gifts, talents, and callings are intended for. Honestly, a lot of the people who are the closest to me have no idea what I really do. They don't know the sacrifices that I make. Honestly, there are people who I love and wholeheartedly support who think that what I do is very miniscule and insignificant compared to what they do. It used to hurt, but not anymore.

There are people in my life who don't get me at all. They misunderstand what I say, they misjudge my intentions, all of that. However, what I am learning is that no amount of misunderstanding should cause you to miss the mark. Those who are supposed to understand will understand. Don't do like I used to do and allow the need to prove yourself and be understood to outweigh the need to BE who you're here to be and DO what you're here to do. Think about Jesus. His disciples didn't really understand it all until He had come and gone. It's like that sometimes. Don't let it get you down. Just know that as you continue to walk out your purpose, the people you are called to will get it. Focus on hitting every mark. Focus on going every place that you're supposed to go. Staying in the same place and marking time while trying to explain to everyone around you who you are and why you're here does a great disservice to the people you're called to.

If I waited until everyone in my life understood me, you wouldn't be reading this book right now. I can PROMISE you that. I had to make the decision to move on with my life and trust God more than I trusted in the approval and validation I thought I needed from others. Every need you have will be supplied... but you can't major in the minors. Shift your focus. God understands.

Enjoy today! Say to yourself, "God knows exactly who I am." LIVE like you know and believe that. #iSpeakLife

✳✳ *Write it Out* ✳✳

How does being misunderstood make you feel? What are some positive affirmations that you can make every day to combat those feelings?

Day Nine:

Come Here, Woman!

"Jesus returned to the Mount of Olives, but early the next morning he was back again at the Temple. A crowd soon gathered, and he sat down and taught them. As he was speaking, the teachers of religious law and the Pharisees brought a woman who had been caught in the act of adultery. They put her in front of the crowd. 'Teacher,' they said to Jesus, 'this woman was caught in the act of adultery. The law of Moses says to stone her. What do you say?' They were trying to trap him into saying something they could use against him, but Jesus stooped down and wrote in the dust with his finger. They kept demanding an answer, so he stood up again and said, 'All right, but let the one who has never sinned throw the first stone!' Then he stooped down again and wrote in the dust.
When the accusers heard this, they slipped away one by one, beginning with the oldest, until only Jesus was left in the middle of the crowd with the woman. Then Jesus stood up again and said to the woman, 'Where are your accusers? Didn't even one of them condemn you?' 'No, Lord,' she said.
And Jesus said, 'Neither do I. Go and sin no more.'"

John 8:1-11 (NLT)

~ Today's Declaration ~

For the rest of my life, I will embody what it is to be favored by God.

Caught... in the very act. I can't tell you how many suicide calls I have received from people who have been caught doing something wrong and later brought to open shame. I can't tell you how many times people have emailed me pictures and blogs that have been posted online and asked me to reach out to the people named in them and make sure that they were alive and well.

We live in a cold world. A lot of people thrive on making an open show of the wrongdoings of others. People will do almost anything for a like, a retweet, and a viral social media story. It's sad. However, it's not new. The same types of things went on in the days of old.

The woman in this passage of scripture was clearly wrong. I would be a fool to say that there was nothing wrong with what she did. She was caught having sex with someone who wasn't her husband. Imagine her embarrassment. Imagine her shame. Imagine how she must have felt knowing that even though it clearly takes two to have sex, SHE would be the one brought before Jesus and the crowd.

People standing around... with hatred in their eyes... Laughing, pointing, scoffing, sneering... rolling their eyes at her... wholeheartedly expressing their disdain... all because someone wants to challenge Jesus and prove a point. It is amazing the lengths that people will go to just to show someone else up.

So they tell Jesus what's going on, and they ask Him what to do, being that by law, the woman is up for a stoning. Jesus does something amazing. He knows that this question is a trap, so he isn't quick to answer it. He gets low... and starts to write in the ground with his finger. What was He writing? WHY was He writing? Of course, by now, the Pharisees are upset because they feel like they are being ignored, so they press Jesus for an answer.

Interestingly enough, Jesus gives them the okay. He tells them that whoever has never sinned can go ahead and cast the first stone, and He gets low again and starts to write in the dirt yet again.

The Bible says that when those who had brought the woman in front of Jesus heard this, they backed away one by one, starting with the oldest. I wonder what Jesus was writing. Maybe He was writing the names of the people who had slept with the woman. Maybe He was writing the sins that the men had committed. Maybe He was writing what the men were thinking. I don't think we'll ever really know... but whatever it was, it was so powerful that when it was all said and done, the Pharisees were gone, and only Jesus remained with the woman and the crowd. He asked her a question: "Where are your accusers?" He asked, "Didn't even one of them condemn you?" She said, "No, Lord." So... Jesus said, "Neither do I. Go and sin no more."

That's grace. That's mercy. It didn't take away the fact that she had sinned. It didn't mean that she hadn't done wrong. But it DID mean that Jesus didn't condemn her. He just told her to go... and to make sure that she didn't repeat her past mistakes.

That's what I'm telling you today. I know that you have done a lot in your lifetime. I have, too. I have cursed, fornicated, stolen, lied, cheated, the list goes on and on and on... but God did not condemn me. Listen. God did not condemn me. God is not condemning you either. This is your moment. This is your chance. Get up... Go... and sin no more. This is it. This is your opportunity to get clean and stay clean. This is your open door to change. Hit the ground running and don't look back. LIVE like you are the recipient of the same grace this woman received... because you are.

We're in Day 9... and I'm proud of you for making it this far. Tell yourself that you can do this. Tell yourself how proud you are of yourself. Think about where you were on Day 1 and where you are now. I KNOW it's getting better. It HAS to be. Let's make this a wonderful day! Let's LIVE. I believe in you. I believe in God's plan for your life. LIVE. #iSpeakLife

❖❖ *Write it Out* ❖❖

Looking at this passage of scripture, think about a time when you behaved like the Pharisees did. If you could relive that moment, what (if anything) would you do differently? Now that you know that you are the recipient of that same grace, how will you live your life?

I Speak Life

Day Ten:

Revenge

"Don't hit back; discover beauty in everyone. If you've got it in you, get along with everybody. Don't insist on getting even; that's not for you to do. 'I'll do the judging,' says God. 'I'll take care of it.' Our Scriptures tell us that if you see your enemy hungry, go buy that person lunch, or if he's thirsty, get him a drink. Your generosity will surprise him with goodness. Don't let evil get the best of you; get the best of evil by doing good."

Romans 12:17-21 The Message (MSG)

~ Today's Declaration ~

My job is not to seek revenge. My job is to learn from the experience and continue to do good deeds.

It can be soooooooooooo hard to turn the other cheek. It can be tough trying to stay calm, cool, and collected. There is nothing worse than being run through the mud by someone and the seeing them go on with their lives like they didn't do you wrong. It's hard to hear them tell their side of the story and totally leave out or greatly diminish their contribution to the situation. It makes you mad. It makes you want to get back at them. It makes you want to tell "the real truth" and clear your name. I totally get it.

Please don't ever think that I'm writing this devotional from a place of cluelessness. Even as I'm sitting here writing this, I'm thinking about a situation that I'm dealing with, and how I am feeling about this person's "selective amnesia". I'm not exempt at all, nor am I perfect, nor am I telling you to do something that I don't have to do myself. Whew! I digress.

So here's the thing: It's not your job to seek revenge. It's not my job either. It's actually a waste of time and energy. I'm not telling you to let people walk all over you, but I AM telling you that plotting and scheming to get someone back just isn't worth it. God handles all. I have seen some crazy stuff go down in my lifetime, and I have learned to rest in the fact that through everything I endure and see, God is right there, handling it all. I don't have to fight, I don't have to get people back, I don't have to do any of that. Everything gets taken care of by the natural processes that God has set in place.

Don't be a vehicle that evil can use to travel. It's not worth it, and you are worth so much more than that. Don't think evil of those who have mistreated you. Wish them well. You don't have to be their best friend, but you can definitely wish them the best in all that they do. Pray that God will continue to bless them. Allow yourself to live in freedom and don't allow yourself to be bound by what others have done to you. It's rough, hunni. I know! God knows I know! But you can do it. I promise. It gets easier and easier the more you do it... and you'll always come out on top because there will be nothing standing between you and the things God has for you.

Yesterday we talked about the woman who was caught in the act of adultery. She could have sought revenge against the men and blasted them in front of Jesus... but why? She had just received grace and mercy. Why would she waste her energy? We want everybody to pay for what they have done to us, and that is understandable - but what if you had to pay for everything that you had done to others? What if NOTHING you EVER did was pardoned? You'd spend your LIFETIME on punishment. It's not up to us to make others suffer like they have made us suffer. Sometimes seeing you rise and thrive is punishment enough. It shows the adversary that alllllll of that planning and allllllll of those attacks against you only made you BETTER! Trust me when I tell you that NO ONE can handle things like God can. Don't worry. Don't try to get people back... Just LIVE... and let live. You'll be happier and your life will be sweeter.

I speak freedom to you. I decree and declare that you will not allow yourself to be driven by the need for revenge. I speak that you will forgive and move on with your life without thinking or speaking evil towards those who have done evil towards you. You WILL overcome evil with good. You WILL. Have a wonderful day today. LIVE. #iSpeakLife

❊❊ *Write it Out* ❊❊

Letting go can be tough if you're not used to doing so. Write out a prayer that you commit to pray every time the wrongdoings of others come across your mind and cause you to want to seek revenge.

Day Eleven:
Why Don't They Love Me?

"The Lord is merciful and gracious, slow to anger and abounding in steadfast love."

Psalm 103:8 (ESV)

~ Today's Declaration ~

My job is not to seek revenge. My job is to learn from the experience and continue to do good deeds.

It is amazing that you could be surrounded by fifty people who love you and still only be focused on the few people who don't. It is amazing that hundreds of people can support you and the work you are doing, but you will still be disheartened over that one person who doesn't support you.

I know that feeling all too well. There are certain people who you expect to always give you the same amount of love that you give them, or at least attempt to give you SOMETHING that resembles love and support. It can be hard to pour out to people and not seem to get that back. It is heartbreaking to see those you love seemingly supporting everyone else in the world but you. Other people could rescue a turtle crossing the road and get a whole public announcement of gratitude and honor, and you could save ten people from a burning building and not even get an honorable mention. I get it. TRUST ME... I completely understand, and I know how those happenings can make someone feel. Things like that contributed greatly to my suicide attempts. I truly get it.

We all want love. We all need love. There is something within all of us that desires to be loved, supported, and valued. Don't ever let anyone tell you any differently. There is a healthy place to be in when it comes to the need of love, but there is also an unhealthy place. Your need for love should never cause you to violate your conscience, your integrity, your standards, morals, or any of that. That's never good. However, don't ever think that your desire to be loved and supported is invalid. It's not. The Bible tells us plainly in several passages that we are to love one another. That's a commandment. It's the greatest gift. It's what we were put here to do and to feel.

I have made some very hard-to-swallow observations over the course of my life. Some people don't love because they don't really know how to love. Some people have never received genuine love, so they can only give the type of love that they have received. Some people have been hurt and violated so much that they are afraid to love. Can I be honest? Some people don't love you because they don't want to. They have reasons... excuses... whatever... but at the end of the day, they just don't want to.

So, let's talk about that. Here's the thing: You can spend the rest of your life trying to earn someone else's love. Literally. I give you permission. You don't need my permission, but in case you feel like you do, here it is. #Permission

But while you're busy doing that, let me tell you what you will miss out on. You will miss out on the love of God that trumps any and everything any and everybody could ever do to show you love. You'll miss out on all of the people in your life who really love you for who you are. You'll miss out on all of the people you would meet later who would love you unconditionally. You'll miss out on making the impact you're supposed to make in the world because you'll be too busy trying to get ONE PERSON to love you.

Oh, I get it. She's your MOM. He's your DAD. Your only BROTHER. Your SISTER. Your BEST FRIEND. You can't make it without their love and support... But here you are... making it... without their love and support.

Maybe they'll come around later. Maybe when you're standing in your greatness, fulfilling your purpose, living your dreams, they will see the error of their ways and come around. Maybe they won't. Listen. I KNOW it's hard... but do not allow your life to hinge upon who loves you and who doesn't. You will waste YEARS of your time that you will NEVER GET BACK. You will NEVER reach your full potential if you allow the lack of love and support from others to hold you back. EVER. You wouldn't be reading this book right now if I waited for support from certain people - because I STILL don't have it. But what I DO have is the love of God... and that love is a force that is stronger than any neglect, rejection, disappointment, or ANYTHING ELSE that you and I will ever feel. I promise. When you tap into that love, you'll see things differently. It will still hurt at times, because we still live on this physical plane and see things from a physical perspective, but I promise you that it won't heart nearly as much.

The love of God is GREAT. It's all-encompassing. It's life-saving. It's life-changing. It's unconditional. It's free. I declare that today will be the day that you are hit head-on with the love of

God. Not the love that religion teaches. I'm talking about the raw, uncut, unedited, unfiltered, uncontaminated, true love of God. I decree that today will be the day that you stop worrying about who and what you don't have. I decree that you will focus on the fact that God loves you unconditionally and will make sure that you have what you need to LIVE out what you have been sent here to do. I decree and declare that you will not be bound by a cycle of looking for love in all the wrong places. I pray today that you will gain clarity about who you are and who you belong to. I decree that the effects of rejection will not stunt your growth. You WILL reach your potential. You WILL see the manifestation of what God has spoken over you. And even if you have to walk alone, you WILL hold your head up and you WILL walk into EVERYTHING God has set forth for you. Yep. You will. Now get out there and handle your business! LIVE! #iSpeakLife

❖❖ *Write it Out* ❖❖

List seven things you love about yourself and explain why you love those things.

Day Twelve:

Family

"Keep your heart with all vigilance, for from it flow the springs of life. Put away from you crooked speech, and put devious talk far from you. Let your eyes look directly forward, and your gaze be straight before you. Ponder the path of your feet; then all your ways will be sure. Do not swerve to the right or to the left; turn your foot away from evil."

Proverbs 4:24-27 (ESV)

~ Today's Declaration ~

I will defy the odds.

Family... Family.... Family. We often think that our family members are a different breed of people, but the fact of the matter is that people are people. Our family members are people who happen to have the same blood and chromosomes and stuff - but they're people, nonetheless. So... Whatever you see in the world, whatever you see on reality television, whatever you see on the news, whatever you see at your job, whatever you see on various street corners - trust me when I say that you will see it in your family. That's just how that goes.

I have a cousin who experienced something very traumatic at a young age. Her mother was murdered right in front of her. As a result of this tragedy, she (along with her siblings) went through a lot of things in life that probably would have turned out differently had this tragedy not occurred. I can remember seeing her walking the street and wanting to turn my nose up like so many others did who knew her and her siblings. I remember my grandma saying to me, "You better not ever look down on her. She's your family. She has a heart just like everybody else. You better not talk about her." My grandma went on and on and on about it... but it taught me something.

Anything that happens to someone else could have easily happened to me. I could have been a child molester. I could have been a murderer. I could have been a robber. I could have been a gang member. I could have been a drug addict. I could have been an alcoholic. You name it - any of those things could have happened to me. I'm no different than the people in my family that some would be ashamed of. The only difference is that life dealt me a different hand. Same deck of cards. Same kings, queens, aces, jacks, numbers... Same spades, clubs, diamonds, and hearts... Same deck of cards. Just different hands. That's all.

Stop being ashamed of your family members. Stop letting secrets and fear and shame come between you and your family. The same way that "so and so" from the soap opera is the way that he or she is because of what happened to them in childhood, that same thing also applies to that person in your family who is that way. We're all people. We all have stories. We all have issues. Your family members are no different. They're not perfect. Neither are you. You don't have to be best friends with them. But the moment you realize that they are people just like the people you see at Walmart, Target, or whoever else you go… That's the moment that you will realize that you don't need to expect them to be anyone or anything but who they are.

You may not want to admit that you came from "that family", but you did. You may not want to admit that the lady they see walking up and down the street looking for a hit is your mother, but she is. She's a person like the next person you see walking up and down the street. She may be an ace and the other person may be a spade… but it's the same deck of cards. Don't be ashamed. If anything, be proud that God chose you to rise above the circumstances your family members may have presently succumbed to. Have you seen Jesus' family? Did you read about His lineage? There's a prostitute in there. There's a liar and a trickster in there. There's a murderer in there. But… Jesus came through all of that. So did you. Appreciate that. Use what you know to go back and bring healing to those God chose to connect you to by blood. Don't let it define you. Let it strengthen you to be able to walk boldly into who and what God has created you to be.

Your life isn't predicated on your family history. It's predicated on the will of God. Jesus still came and did everything He was supposed to do. Where He came from was just that - where He came from. It didn't stop him. Yeah, they laughed at him for being "the carpenter's son", but that didn't stop him from healing the sick and raising the dead. EVERYTHING about your life and history has gone into making you who you are. There's no condemnation for that. You were born out of an incestuous relationship? Okay. You're here now. What are you gonna do? Your mom had you by a married man who was not hers? Okay.

That got you here. Now what? What are you going to do? Your family isn't your "real family"? They adopted you? Okay. But you're here. What are you gonna do? Jesus' earthly daddy wasn't His daddy. He still did what He had to do.

Come on... This is YOUR LIFE. The present is YOUR GIFT. NOW. Right now. What are you going to do? I know what I'm going to do. I'm going to LIVE. I'm going to rise above it ALL. I'm going to break EVERY generational curse. I'm going to leave MY MARK on this planet. That's what I'm gonna do. I encourage you to do the same. Let's go. NOW. #iSpeakLife

❖❖ *Write it Out* ❖❖

Think of one family member that you have been ashamed of. Why are you ashamed of that person? What will you do from this day forward to show that person love and acceptance?

Day Thirteen:

I-95

"The thief does not come except to steal, and to kill, and to destroy. I have come that they may have life, and that they may have it more abundantly."

John 10:10 (NKJV)

~ Today's Declaration ~

I will not die before my time.

So... Today is the day that I give you a glimpse into one of my suicide attempts. NO shame. ***DISCLAIMER*** Please do not try this at home. This is my personal testimony, and I am sharing it strictly for that purpose. I will not be held liable for any attempt to replicate this situation or any other situation mentioned in this book.

Here we go.

I was nineteen years old. I was dealing with a lot of brokenness and rejection. I didn't seem to be good enough for anyone in my life, and I was constantly being verbally abused all in the name of "holiness" and "living right". I didn't seem to fit in, and I was constantly being stabbed in the back by people in my life, yet my need for love seemed to keep me going around the same circles with these same people... because hey, somehow, they really loved me... right?

I digress.

So, I was leaving a church service. I won't go into the details of what happened in the service, but let's just say that I was publicly bashed by several people. I was angry, hurt, disappointed, and so much more. I remember driving down the highway with hot tears streaming down my face, and I remember telling God that this was it. I was at the end of my rope. I had done all I knew to do, and nothing had worked. I had never felt so lost in all of my life.

I remember driving down the road and looking in the rear view mirror and seeing a silhouette of a man sitting in the back of my car. I'll never forget what I heard his voice say. He said, "You really should go into that oncoming traffic over there. No one will care. They won't even look for you. You don't matter to anyone but yourself." Over and over again, that's what I heard.

The tears grew hotter and fell faster... more and more... more and more. The voice intensified. I wanted to scream, but the scream never made it past my throat. My car started to go faster and faster. I wanted someone, anyone... to help me... but there was nothing I could say. My car went even faster.

I remember telling myself that the only way I'd be able to stop this fight in my mind would be to just end my life. I wasn't sold on the idea because I wondered what would happen if I died but the fight continued... so I kept driving. I looked down at my speedometer. 104 miles per hour. Driving down I-95.

I saw a weigh station up ahead, and I knew that a lot of transfer trucks would be coming onto the highway... I began to veer over from one lane to the next lane. I paid no attention to whether or not any cars were coming up behind me. I just changed lanes. From the far lane on my side, I just had to pick a good time to go over to the other side of the highway.

I remember thinking about everyone that I was about to leave behind, and all I could think about was the fact that so many people had treated me so badly... I was a KID. I didn't know what I was doing in life. I wasn't trying to hurt anyone. I wasn't trying to cause anyone any trouble. I just had a hard time figuring things out sometimes. That was all. More tears.

"Okay. This is it. Whatever happens, happens." I let go.

I let go of the steering wheel. I let go of my emotions. I let the tears fall. I let the screams come out. I begged God to forgive me and to let me "make it in" even though I was going about it in this terrible and catastrophic manner. My car began to shift to the left. I went over the rumble strips. I went into the shoulder. I went into the grass.

My car slowed down.

I pressed the gas.... I stomped on the gas pedal. My car kept slowing down. There I was... In the grass... at a complete stop. I looked up and saw all of the transfer trucks coming. I could see a few of the drivers' faces. They were slowing down a little bit to make sure that I was okay.

I got out of the car... I kicked it... and I cried. I cried out all of the tears that I had been holding in that day. I cried because I wanted to die. I cried because I wanted to live. I cried because I was tired of the pain. I cried because I wanted things to change. I cried because I thought I was crazy. I cried because I was still alive... I cried because I didn't know what to do. I screamed. I punched my car. I cried.

Standing there on that grass, I realized something. I realized that God was with me. I realized that my life had been spared. And then, I REALLY cried. I cried because I had been given another chance.

That wasn't my last suicide attempt, but it was one of the ones that allowed me to see and understand that God is greater than anything we face, and that when God speaks life, all you can do is LIVE. You can't go before your time. God will ALWAYS intervene. I wanted to die that night. God didn't want me to. I didn't.

Listen. It's rough out here. Sometimes it may seem like it would be better if you weren't here. It may seem like there is a better life waiting for you on the other side and that you may as well go on over there. I get it. If this world is so bad, why can't you just leave when you want to, right? I get it. But... Listen. God placed you here for a reason. If you leave here right now, you'll never know what all of your pain was for. You'll never understand why you had to go through what you went through in your childhood. You'll never understand why you had to suffer like you suffered. You'll never get your reward. Listen to me. I know that you may feel like it doesn't matter at this point, but it does. That's why you have made it to day thirteen of this devotional. It's not your time to die.

As I said at the beginning of this book, I have attempted suicide over twenty-two times. Each attempt was surrounded by its own set of horrible circumstances. However, God did not see fit to let me leave there, because God knew that there was a purpose for the things I endured.

HONESTLY SPEAKING, if I went through all of that just to be able to write this book and make it available so that it could reach you and you could read it and decide against suicide, then nothing I went through was in vain. NOTHING. That's what you have to understand. All of this has purpose. There is someone sitting somewhere waiting for you to come through what you're going through. There's a little boy somewhere who has been molested that is just waiting to hear your story so that he can know that his story doesn't have to end with that molestation. There is a woman who just finished being abused who is sitting there knowing that there must be someone somewhere who can help her.

What you have gone through is not in vain. You may not want to see whether or not there is a light at the end of the tunnel, but I am here to tell you that God is walking with you through this tunnel, and God is waiting for you at the other side where the light is. Trust God.

I speak peace to you. I speak sweet peace to you. I speak clarity and wisdom. I decree and declare that you will have a new appreciation for your life. I pray that God will begin to allow you to share your story with all who need to hear it. I come against the spirit that would try to cause you to give up. I come against the longing you have had to want to escape your life. I bind that spirit. You will LIVE. You WILL LIVE. YOU WILL LIVE. You will not die before your time. You will not jump off a bridge. You will not wreck your car. You will not cut yourself. You will not overdose. You will not die before your time. You will LIVE. LIVE, LIVE, LIVE, LIVE, LIVE, LIVE, LIVE.

TODAY. You will live today. I decree that. The enemy will not be able to get into your mind and cause you to want to give up on life. You will LIVE. Go in peace. LIVE today. #iSpeakLife

✷ *Write it Out* ✷

You're in a room. A man walks in and says, "I'll pay you for your value if you can convince me of your worth." What would you say?

Day Fourteen:

Knives in Your Back

"And as they were reclining at table and eating, Jesus said, 'Truly, I say to you, one of you will betray me, one who is eating with me.' They began to be sorrowful and to say to him one after another, 'Is it I?' He said to them, 'It is one of the twelve, one who is dipping bread into the dish with me.'"

Mark 14:18-21 (ESV)

~ Today's Declaration ~

I am stronger because of what I have endured.

We have all experienced betrayal. It hurts. I think it's safe to say that we have all betrayed someone before, too. That hurt them as well.

Betrayal is something that cuts like a knife. There is nothing like giving someone your trust and loyalty and being stabbed in the back. The pain of knives in your back is a different kind of pain. It's a pain that stings AND aches. It's rough.

Let's look at today's scripture passage. Jesus is sitting at the table with the people HE PICKED to walk with Him through life. They're sitting down, chilling, having a nice meal, and Jesus breaks the news that someone siting there eating with them is going to betray Him.

Imagine that. I'm sure the whispers started. I'm sure that EVERYONE had their suspicions. The bible says that everyone became sorrowful and asked if they were "the one". Jesus just let them know again that it was one of them who was breaking bread with him that night.

Jesus knew ahead of time that Judas was going to betray Him, but He didn't let that change His treatment of Judas. Unlike Jesus, we don't always know ahead of time who is going to betray us. As a matter of fact, sometimes we don't even see it coming. It hurts… Oh, how it hurts.

By now, you should know where this is going. Yes. It hurts. However, it does not have to define you. It doesn't have to end your life. You can move on. You can live through it. Just make sure that while you're living and moving on, you learn the lesson you're supposed to learn.

Now that we've gotten that out of the way, I want to talk about a different type of betrayal. Here's a little bit of knowledge for you. Every time you try to harm yourself, you are betraying who you really are. You are taking a knife and stabbing yourself in the back. That's what you do every time you affirm negativity about yourself. Here you are, trying your best to make it through life, and then you say out of your mouth, "I'll NEVER make it." That's betrayal. Here you are, trying to forgive, and you say out of your mouth, "I'm not forgiving him/her." Betrayal. You know that your body is the temple of the Holy Ghost, but because you're upset about your current situation, you do something damaging to your body. Betrayal.

You can't get mad at someone for betraying you when you constantly betray yourself. You're putting "It's okay to betray me" into the atmosphere every time you do those things to yourself. I'm not telling you anything I haven't had to walk through myself. The purpose of this book isn't to focus on others and what they have done to you. The purpose of this book is for you to focus on YOU and the amazing and victorious life that YOU are destined to have. Once you deal with how you are hurting yourself, you'll find that others can't hurt you so easily.

TODAY... I want you to let go of those feelings you have towards those who have betrayed you. Think about the story of Joseph in Genesis 37. Had his brothers never betrayed him, he never would have made it to the palace. Even with Jesus, had Judas never betrayed Him, how would He have made it to the cross? Trust me when I say that EVERYTHING happens for a reason. LIVE like you know that. Every betrayal serves as a catalyst to propel you into something greater. LIVE like you know that.

You are not a victim. You are victorious. Count it all joy. It's really okay. Come on. Let's get those knives out of your back. Let's get cleaned up. We've got some LIVING to do. #iSpeakLife

❖ *Write it Out* ❖

What would you say to someone who has been betrayed? Keep your writing for future reference.

Na'Kole Watson

Day Fifteen:

Pillows Over Your Face

"When the righteous cry for help, the Lord hears and delivers them out of all their troubles. The Lord is near to the brokenhearted and saves the crushed in spirit. Many are the afflictions of the righteous, but the Lord delivers him out of them all. He keeps all his bones; not one of them is broken."

Psalm 34: 17-20 (ESV)

~ Today's Declaration ~

I have come entirely too far to give up or turn around.

I'm sure you know what it's like to struggle to breathe. It's not a good feeling at all. I wrote a poem entitled, "My Suicide" (you can view it by going to vimeo.com/90441322). In the video, I talk about my suicide attempts and what caused them. I'm going to talk about another one today. Again, please see the disclaimer from Day 13. It applies here, and everywhere that I talk about my suicide attempts.

I had cried myself to sleep. I had grown very close my classmate's mom. My classmate was graduating, which meant that her mom wouldn't really be working with the marching band anymore. I was so very sad about this. I cried every time I had to leave her. We were VERY CLOSE. I talked to her EVERY DAY. When we would come back home from band trips, I would go and sit in the seat with her and lay in her lap or on her chest. She encouraged me, she motivated me… She was ALWAYS there for me when I needed someone to talk to.

I had another classmate/bandmate who I confided in. I told her how sad I was about this lady leaving, and I said that I was "lovestruck". Boy oh boy. I didn't mean that I was in love with this woman. I didn't mean that at all. I was a sad teenager using the first word that came to mind.

So. To make a long story short, the girl told the lady, the lady's daughter, and pretty much the whole marching band what I had said. We had a trip that weekend (our last trip, which prompted my feelings), and I noticed that she (the lady) was not talking to me AT ALL. She wouldn't even make eye contact with me. We got to the band trip and when I walked up to the bleachers, one of the drummers said, "Hey, it's _____" and made reference to a transgender person from a movie. That's when it hit me. I don't think I will ever forget that. That's when I put two and two together, and realized that I had been betrayed.

I cried all the way home. I cried myself to sleep. I woke up in the middle of the night, and I got all of my pillows… I laid my face in my sheets, I pushed my pillows over my head, and I used my arms and palms to try to suffocate myself. Right at the point that I should have blacked out, I would start kicking and gasping, and my hands would get weak. I know I tried at least twenty times. Same result each time.

Listen to me. There is something within ALL of us that will fight for our lives. Even when people die by hanging, they often have marks around their neck from where they tried to escape the grasp of the rope or belt or whatever mechanism they used. As much as I wanted to die, God put something in me that wanted us to live. Science shows that we have a natural reflex that kicks in at moments like these. It's actually pretty amazing. I owe God my life because God spared my life so many times… God held it together for me when I didn't even think I wanted it to be held together. I'm grateful.

I know that being misunderstood is hard. Suffering betrayal is hard. Being lonely is hard. I know it is. It's hard having to cry every day. It's hard trying to get people to accept you. Being left out is hard. Being constantly criticized is hard. It's painful. Life brings us pain. Life can be almost unbearable sometimes. I know. I know… I know… But let me tell you something. GOD… has brought you entirely too far for you to give up.

Guess what! You have now completed half of this journey. You're still here. You have had some good days. You've had some rough days. You've wrestled with some things. But you are still here. You're still here! You can't turn around now. You CANNOT give up now. From here, it only gets better. I decree that for you. It will only get better. Even when it seems hard, you'll know that it's getting better.

Take those pillows off your head. Those pillows of doubt, shame, fear, unforgiveness, anger, bitterness… Get those pillows off of your face. You are supposed to put pillows UNDER your head. You are supposed to position yourself ABOVE them, and they are supposed to bring you comfort and help you to sleep with ease. Yeah, I doubted myself, but now I rest easy because I don't doubt myself anymore. That season of doubt helped me to learn to believe. That shame? Yeah I'm over that. I rest easy at night because I know that I don't have to be ashamed of anything that I have endured. That's behind me. By the end of this book, I decree and declare that you will have the same testimony.

Come on... Let's go. We've got some LIVING to do. Are you ready? I think you are. I'm pulling for you. I'm cheering you forward. #iSpeakLife

❖❖ *Write it Out* ❖❖

What would you do if you weren't afraid? What would you do if you KNEW that you would not fail? Write it down, read it, and tell yourself: "I can do this." You can.

Day Sixteen:

Too Late?

"Now when Jesus returned, the crowd welcomed him, for they were all waiting for him. And there came a man named Jairus, who was a ruler of the synagogue. And falling at Jesus' feet, he implored him to come to his house, for he had an only daughter, about twelve years of age, and she was dying. As Jesus went, the people pressed around him. And there was a woman who had had a discharge of blood for twelve years, and though she had spent all her living on physicians, she could not be healed by anyone. She came up behind him and touched the fringe of his garment, and immediately her discharge of blood ceased. And Jesus said, 'Who was it that touched me?' When all denied it, Peter said, 'Master, the crowds surround you and are pressing in on you!' But Jesus said, 'Someone touched me, for I perceive that power has gone out from me.' And when the woman saw that she was not hidden, she came trembling, and falling down before him declared in the presence of all the people why she had touched him, and how she had been immediately healed. And he said to her, 'Daughter, your faith has made you well; go in peace.' While he was still speaking, someone from the ruler's house came and said, 'Your daughter is dead; do not trouble the Teacher any more.' But Jesus on hearing this answered him, 'Do not fear; only believe, and she will be well.' And when he came to the house, he allowed no one to enter with him, except Peter and John and James, and the father and mother of the child. And all were weeping and mourning for her, but he said, 'Do not weep, for she is not dead but sleeping.' And they laughed at him, knowing that she was dead. But taking her by the hand he called, saying, 'Child, arise.' And her spirit returned, and she got up at once. And he directed that something should be given her to eat.

And her parents were amazed, but he charged them to tell no one what had happened."

Luke 8:40-56 (ESV)

~ Today's Declaration ~

I know that God is not finished.

I've told you a lot about myself over the last few days. Now, I'm going to tell you a little bit about two things that were happening at the same time in this passage of scripture.

Enter Jairus. He's upset because his daughter was dying. This was his only daughter, and you know how men can be about their daughters. He's begging Jesus to come and make everything alright with his princess. I can only imagine his distress as he approached Jesus. He had to be very sad, anxious, and maybe even a little angry.

Jesus is still walking, and there are people EVERYWHERE. The paparazzi had NOTHING on this. People were EVERYWHERE. Among the crowd, there was a woman who had been suffering with "female problems" for twelve years. She had spent everything she had. She had gone from doctor to doctor to doctor, and no one could help her. There she was, actively bleeding, walking in the crowd, trying to get to Jesus. I can imagine her saying that if she could just touch the hem of His clothes, she would be okay. She had just that much faith.

So she pressed through the crowd. I'm sure that people were laughing at her. They may have even told her that she was stinking. They may have spit on her... They could have even pushed her out of the way. She kept pressing. She kept pressing. Through all of the noise, the people, the sways of the crowd going back and forth through the streets... She pressed.

She made it. She touched His clothes. It got His attention. He felt some of His power leaving Him and being transferred to her. He asked who it was that had touched him. Of course, His disciples didn't know. How could they know? There were people on top of people on top of people trying to touch Jesus. How could they know?

Somehow... Somehow... Somehow.

Somehow, the lady looked up and she was in the spotlight. She was no longer hidden in the crowd. She fell at Jesus' feet and began to tell Him of her struggles and of how she was now healed. He told her that her faith had made her whole, and He told her to go in peace.

She had struggled with this issue for twelve years. That's 4,380 days. That's a long time. Goodness gracious. But... As you see, it wasn't too late for her. Every doctor had failed her. There was nothing that any of them could do. However, that didn't mean that it was too late for her to get her healing.

But wait.... What about the little princess? What happened to her?

In this moment, Jairus gets the word that his daughter has died. There he was, begging Jesus to heal his child, and Jesus got "sidetracked" by this woman, and she was healed (congratulations), but what about his kid?

Jesus goes to where the child is and tells Jairus and his family not to worry or be scared... because the girl was only sleeping. Those surrounding Him thought that was funny. They were convinced that she was dead. He takes the girl by the hand and tells her to arise. Her spirit comes back into her body, and she wakes up.

Two situations. Same Jesus. Same faith. Same power. Let me tell you something. I don't care who has given up on you. I don't care who has told you that it was too late. I don't care how many outstanding loans you have. I don't care how bad your credit score is. I don't care how many times you've been turned down. IT IS NOT TOO LATE. I decree that you will rise up in the power of God the same way this woman did. I pray that the right spirit will return to you just like the little girl's spirit returned to her. I decree and declare that this will be the day that you make strides towards handling your unfinished business and reaching your goals. THIS is the day that you will realize that it is NEVER too late. God is with you. God is breathing life into you. God has given you another day. It is NOT too late to LIVE.

Tomorrow. Same time, same place. #iSpeakLife

❖❖ *Write it Out* ❖❖

Go back and get those things you thought you had missed out on. What have you been putting off because you thought it was too late? Start planning today! Let's get it all done!

Na'Kole Watson

Day Seventeen:
The Point of No Return

"Now there were four men who were lepers at the entrance to the gate. And they said to one another, 'Why are we sitting here until we die? If we say, 'Let us enter the city,' the famine is in the city, and we shall die there. And if we sit here, we die also. So now come, let us go over to the camp of the Syrians. If they spare our lives we shall live, and if they kill us we shall but die.' So they arose at twilight to go to the camp of the Syrians. But when they came to the edge of the camp of the Syrians, behold, there was no one there. For the Lord had made the army of the Syrians hear the sound of chariots and of horses, the sound of a great army, so that they said to one another, 'Behold, the king of Israel has hired against us the kings of the Hittites and the kings of Egypt to come against us.' So they fled away in the twilight and abandoned their tents, their horses, and their donkeys, leaving the camp as it was, and fled for their lives. And when these lepers came to the edge of the camp, they went into a tent and ate and drank, and they carried off silver and gold and clothing and went and hid them. Then they came back and entered another tent and carried off things from it and went and hid them."

II Kings 7:3-8 (ESV)

~ Today's Declaration ~

What is the point of no return? When you're on a journey, the point of no return is the place you make it to when it's no longer feasible to turn around, and the only thing that makes sense is to continue on to your destination. It's that part in your road trip when it would take more gas and miles and time to go back than it would to continue on to your destination. It's that part in your research paper when although you may not like everything you have written, it would make more sense to just finish the paper than to start all over.

That's where we are.

Day 17.

It makes no sense to turn around at this point. Yeah, we still have several days to go. Yeah, you still have some of the same stuff going on. Nope, your life isn't ideal yet. Yeah, you may still feel like ending it all sometimes. Yep, those family members still get on your nerves. Forgiving folks isn't as easy as you thought it would be. Nope, it's not.

You still have bills. You didn't win the lottery. Your boss is still getting on your nerves. Kids are acting the monkey. Peace? Yeah, in fleeting moments. It's not what you thought it would be. Your life hasn't changed as quickly as you thought. You're wondering if you should even finish this devotional. You thought this was going to help you. You don't feel helped.

I get it.

But this is Day 17. And at this point, it would make more sense to continue than it would to turn around. Let me tell you about these lepers.

They were presented with an opportunity. They couldn't function among the citizens of the town, because they were LEPERS. They were unclean. They couldn't mingle with the regular people.

They were at the gate, and they had a decision to make. If they sat there, they were going to die. Hands down. No doubt about it. If they went to the city, they would die, because there was a famine in the city. They didn't really know what would happen if they went to the camp of the Syrians. It was possible that they would die there, too.

These lepers weren't born at the gate. Their journey had brought them to the gate. That gate life wasn't working for them, though. Sound familiar? You didn't just wake up one day and say, "Today I believe I'll struggle with suicidal thoughts. Today I'll try to end my life." You didn't do that. You didn't just randomly buy this devotional because you had nothing better to do with your life. Your journey led you here.

You already know what's behind you. You already know how the story ends if you go the way you were going before. You already know what you will continue to struggle with if you don't put this work in. You already know. It's not changing. It will be just like it was before you picked up this book.

Now, I can't guarantee you that your life will change overnight. I can speak in faith and believe that God will continue to do what seems impossible for you. I can pray that you will be strengthened and restored, I can do all of that... I can finish writing these next thirteen entries, not knowing what the outcome of the publishing of this book will even be (and that's what I'm going to do) … but what are you going to do? Are you gonna just stop right here at the gate? You can't go back to the city. Well you can, but you already know what will happen when you get here. You can sit at the gate, but you already know what is going to happen while you sit there.

What will you do? I'm not making a declaration today. Today, YOU will make the declaration. This is it. What will you do? #iSpeakLife

✻ *Write it Out* ✻

Write whatever is in your heart. Be transparent. Be honest. Let it out.

Day Eighteen:

Darkness

"The earth was without form and void, and darkness was over the face of the deep. And the Spirit of God was hovering over the face of the waters.

Genesis 1:2 (ESV)

"The people stood far off, while Moses drew near to the thick darkness where God was."

Exodus 20:21 (ESV)

~ Today's Declaration ~

The darkness I see and feel is there for my development. God will make everything beautiful when the time comes.

Darkness. We associate it with crime. We associate it with evil. We associate it with bad things and bad things. We fail to realize that God is in the darkness. The darkness isn't always there to harm us. Sometimes, actually, most times, the darkness actually works for your good.

Let me prove my point. You know that there is light at the end of the tunnel because it is dark in the tunnel. So, without that darkness, what significance would the light have? What would be the joy of getting to the end of the tunnel?

I'll take us further. In the beginning, all there was... was God, an earth that hadn't been completely formed, a large amount of water... and darkness. That's all there was. God's Spirit was hovering over the waters... in the darkness.

Out of that darkness, God spoke light. Out of that darkness... FROM that darkness... God spoke into existence everything that exists right now. That's amazing.

Let's get to the natural for a moment. Picture yourself standing in a room and looking at a beautiful photograph of the prettiest landscape you have ever seen. Now I'm gonna take us back a few decades before digital photography emerged.

Let me tell you how that photo in that room was processed. The photographer took the photo. Then, he/she took it into a darkroom. Darkrooms are specifically created to keep light out. It has to be this way in order for the photographs to properly develop, and for the chemicals on the paper not to be "contaminated" by the light. Sounds totally backwards, right? But some of the best photos you have ever seen... were developed... in the dark.

What is God developing in your darkness? Who will you be when you emerge? Let me tell you about my darkness. During my darkness, God was developing me... giving me what I would need to run a suicide prevention, anti-bullying, and social advocacy organization. God was showing me how it felt to be rejected so that I could talk about it in this book. God was allowing me to be betrayed so that I could answer my phone and talk someone out of suicide after they had been betrayed. God allowed me to go through family issues so that I could tell you to keep going in spite of them. God was fortifying me and strengthening me so that when I came out of my season of being suicidal, I would be empowered to make it through writing this book.

Since I started this book, I have seen a lot of darkness. I have cried while writing this book because there are people I'd love to share it with that I can't even talk about it to because they constantly discredit me or act like what I'm doing doesn't matter. I've been overlooked time after time in many instances while I've been writing this book. I've been made to feel like my feelings don't matter at all when I've gone to loved ones and told them how they make me feel. It has been dark. But here I am, right now, sitting on my couch, listening to music... writing to YOU. Here I am. This book is being developed in darkness. Countless people will know that there is hope because of the darkness that I've experienced in my life.

So I'll ask you again: What is God developing in your darkness? That's your "write it out" for today. Trust me. You may not think you know, but if you sit still and listen, you'll know. #iSpeakLife

❖❖ *Write it Out* ❖❖

What is God developing in your darkness?

Day Nineteen:

When Your Pillar Falls

"After the death of Moses the servant of the Lord, the Lord said unto Joshua the son of Nun, Moses' assistant, 'Moses my servant is dead. Now therefore arise, go over this Jordan, you and all this people, into the land that I am giving to them, to the people of Israel. Every place that the sole of your foot will tread upon I have given to you, just as I promised to Moses. From the wilderness and this Lebanon as far as the great river, the river Euphrates, all the land of the Hittites to the Great Sea toward the going down of the sun shall be your territory. No man shall be able to stand before you all the days of your life. Just as I was with Moses, so shall I be with you. I will not leave you or forsake you.'"

Joshua 1:1-5 (ESV)

~ Today's Declaration ~

Though my life has changed, it is still worth living.

On December 15, 2010, my grandma died. I felt like my whole world came tumbling down. When you go from having someone every day of your life for twenty-six years to not having them at all (in the flesh), it is horrible. Two or three of my suicide attempts occurred shortly after my grandmother's death. That was a hard thing for me to endure. It took me months to even realize that she was never coming back in the physical form. MONTHS. It was bad.

When your pillar falls, it is hard. There isn't another word I can use to describe it. But let me tell you what I learned from that experience.

If you have a building that you believe is built on a pillar, and that pillar falls, and the building remains standing, that means that the building wasn't built to be solely dependent upon that particular pillar. There is something else keeping that building together.

That's what God was trying to get Joshua to see. Yes, Moses was dead. Gone. However, there was still work to be done. There was still territory to claim. So God broke it down to Joshua. The same promises that God made Moses applied to Joshua. The same things that God was going to give Moses, God promised to give to Joshua.

The same thing goes for the situation my grandmother's transition. The same way that God took care of my grandma, God would take care of me. As a matter of fact, God was taking care of me THROUGH my grandma the whole time. She was a pillar in my life who supported me until I could get to the place that I understood that my building wasn't solely dependent upon one person. God is the framework of my building. People come and go. No matter who it is, no matter how much they love you, no matter how much you love them - people come and go. It's life. It happens.

Today, I encourage you to shift your perspective. Understand that the same God that was with Moses remained with Joshua. The same promises that Moses had, Joshua had. The same provision that Moses had, Joshua had. None of the goodness that Joshua was to experience was solely because of Moses. It was all because of God. As long as there is a God, your building will NEVER crumble. EVER. Believe that. LIVE. It's okay. It's okay to move forward. It's okay to walk in your promises. You're free to do so. #iSpeakLife

❖ *Write it Out* ❖

Think of someone who is no longer in your life (either by death or by the ending of a relationship). Name something that they taught you that you will always carry with you, and write about how God used that person in your life.

Day Twenty:

Bullies

"Some people make cutting remarks, but the words of the wise bring healing."

Proverbs: 12:18 (ESV)

~ Today's Declaration ~

I will not let anyone's negativity affect my positivity.

As you know, I am the founder of an organization that deals with bullying. I see it every day. Kids are cruel. Teachers are cruel. Parents are cruel. Not all people are cruel, but we have to be honest about the fact that there are lots of cruel people in this world. Some of them bully others to make themselves feel better about their worth. Some bully others because they have been bullied before. There are so many reasons why people do what they do. None of the reasons justify the actions, but there is definitely no shortage of reasons.

Words hurt. That whole "sticks and stones" thing is a myth. You get over physical blows. Cuts heal... but words? Words endure long after the blood stops flowing. Words endure long after the swelling goes down. Words HURT.

I can't tell you that you won't ever be bullied again. I can't tell you that you won't ever be verbally abused. I can't tell you that you won't ever be pushed around (physically or with words) by those who feel like they are superior to you. If I did, I would be misleading you. Greatly.

However, I can tell you that the best way to counteract words is with words. As we see in this scripture, yes, there are people who will constantly say hurtful things. In the midst of this, you have a great opportunity. You have the opportunity to use wisdom and to use your words to bring healing.

You may think you don't know how to do this, but I'm pretty sure that you do. Even if you don't, let me share something with you. The Bible says in James 1:5 (New Living Translation), " If you need wisdom, ask our generous God, and he will give it to you. He will not rebuke you for asking." There's no excuse for you to not be able to do this. Ready? Here we go.

For every negative thing that has been spoken over you, to you, and/or around you, you have the power within you to speak a word to counteract and cancel out what has been said. It HAS to work. It's law. If someone makes a cutting remark, but the words of the wise bring healing, that means that the words of the wise bring healing to the cutting remark, thus making the cutting remark null and void.

I do every day. I could write a whole entire series of books about the things that have been said to me. That's why (and if you follow me on social media, you know this) I try my best and hardest to only affirm good things. I believe that what we speak over ourselves becomes law, and I refuse to legislate anything that is going to bring me down. That's that betrayal we talked about on Day 14. Make a decision today that even in the midst of those words that hurt you, you will stand in your power and speak something different.

I decree that every negative word that has been spoken will be canceled out by something positive that you speak today. I declare that you will no longer use your tongue to speak negativity into the atmosphere about yourself or others. I speak new life to the words that come out of your mouth. May they be words that edify and not words that tear down. I decree and declare that your words will begin to build a new life full of peace and prosperity for you and those connected to you. It takes work, but it can be done. It WILL be done. It SHALL be done. Start today. #iSpeakLife

❖ *Write it Out* ❖

What are some things you can say to counteract the negative things that have been spoken to you?

Day Twenty-One:

Secrets

"And he said to them, 'Is a lamp brought in to be put under a basket, or under a bed, and not on a stand? For nothing is hidden except to be made manifest; nor is anything secret except to come to light.'"

Mark 4:21-22 (ESV)

~ Today's Declaration ~

I will not allow secrets to run nor ruin my life.

Secrets. They eat away at us. Every time we get ready to lift our hands in worship, they are there. Every time we get ready to move forward, they are there. When we meet someone new, yep - secrets are right there.

So many people have attempted and/or committed suicide because of secrets either being revealed or rising to the surface and almost coming to the light. It's a terrible thing.

Today isn't about telling all of your secrets. There are some things that I have experienced, done, said, etc. that I will NEVER tell. They will go with me to my grave, urn, the river, or wherever my remains end up. I will NEVER tell a soul. There are some secrets that I have HAD to tell in order to get free from the condemnation and shame surrounding them. It goes both ways.

I can't make the decision for you. It's not my place. I'm not telling you to tell anything, and I am not telling you to keep anything. What I'm telling you is that there isn't a single thing hidden that won't be revealed. That doesn't necessarily mean that all of your secrets will become known to the world. It means that your secrets will be revealed to YOU. YOU will have to deal with them.

There are things that happen in childhood that we "bury"... but have you ever noticed that the thing you thought was buried still comes up from time to time? It could come up when you hear a voice that sounds like the voice of someone who assaulted or molested you. It could come up when you smell a scent that reminds you of the person you had an affair with. It could come up when you hear a baby crying. There are so many ways that these things come up.

These things don't come up to torment us. That may be the enemy's intention, but remember that God's intentions will always trump the intentions of the enemy, and according to Jeremiah 29:11, God thinks thoughts of peace and not evil towards us. These things come up so that we can properly deal with them.

I encourage you to deal with your secrets. Even if it's no more than saying, "God, I did this. I am sorry that I did this. I forgive myself." or "God, I have been living in guilt and shame because this happened to me. Today I want to be free from that guilt and shame." - I encourage you to do that. I encourage you to free yourself.

Let me forewarn you: When you do this, the emotions WILL COME. Every emotion that you have held back in regards to these secrets WILL MANIFEST. You have to let them come. That's a part of the healing process. Don't just let them come, though. Let them come AND GO. Feel them… embrace them… tell yourself why you're feeling what you're feeling. Give it to God. It's gotta stay in motion. You can't sit still on any of those steps. You can't wallow in any of those emotions. You have to let them come and go. No matter how good or how bad they are, you have to let them come and go. That's the only way to get free.

I have faith that you can do this. It's going to be tough at times. You may even need to reach out to someone to help you through it. That's okay. There's a whole section of resources in the back of this book. I would rather see you crying for a moment than see you bound for a lifetime. I come against every spirit of anxiety, depression, and fear. You can do this. Live. I believe in you. #iSpeakLife

** *Write it Out* **

How do you plan to carry out the action plan discussed in today's devotional? Will you do it as the opportunity arises? Will you set aside a special time of healing? What will you do?

Day Twenty-Two:
The Revealer of Hearts

"But the Lord said to Samuel, "Do not look on his appearance or on the height of his stature, because I have rejected him. For the Lord sees not as man sees: man looks on the outward appearance, but the Lord looks on the heart."

1 Samuel 16:7 (ESV)

~ Today's Declaration ~

Today I let go of everything that doesn't serve a good purpose in my life.

Saul had been rejected by the Lord. Samuel was commissioned to go and anoint the next king. When he got to Jesse's house, he saw Jesse's son, Eliab, and thought he would be the next king. God wasn't having it, hence today's scripture passage. God doesn't see things as we see them. We see using our physical senses because we exist on the physical plane. God sees far beyond that.

I'll liken it to this: Do you remember that friend, boyfriend, or girlfriend you just LOVED when you were younger? Do you remember your mom, dad, grandma, grandpa, or someone older than you saying, "Nope. They're not the one. They're no good for you." or something of that sort? Do you remember how mad you got? Do you remember how you thought they just didn't know what they were talking about? You thought they were just hating on you. They wouldn't let you be great. Remember? But do you also remember how that person turned out to not be the one? Do you remember how that friend ended up being the total opposite of what you thought he/she was? Do you remember?

If it's like that with our earthly parents and family members, can you imagine how it is with God? God can literally see all the way through you. God can see the atoms bumping into each other. God can SEE. Seriously. God is the revealer of hearts. Don't ignore that. Don't ignore the small voice that says, "No, I wouldn't do that. No, I wouldn't trust them. No, that's not a good idea." Remember. God is the revealer of hearts.

Jesus knew that Judas was going to stab Him in the back. How did He know? Because God is the revealer of hearts. However, Jesus still had to do what He was here to do, even though He already knew how everything would go down with Judas.

When God shows you something, that doesn't mean that you always have to make a scene and issue a big "I'm cutting you off" announcement. That's not wisdom. If you keep reading in I Samuel 16, you'll notice that Samuel just moved on to the next son. That's all. He didn't go into a long monologue about how Eliab wasn't "the one". He just kept going on to the next one. That's what we have to do.

Trust that God sees and knows. Follow that quiet voice you hear within. It may sound like you. It may sound like a familiar voice. Regardless of how it sounds, if you belong to God, you know the voice of God. You wouldn't be reading this book if you didn't belong to God. So, that lets us both know that you know the voice of God. Trust it.

God, we thank You for being the revealer of hearts. Help us to trust Your voice. Help us to trust not only what You reveal to us about others, but ESPECIALLY what You reveal to us about OURSELVES.

Everything that isn't serving a good purpose has to go. Be led by God. Don't be led by your emotions. Don't be led by the desire to please others. Be led by God. Make the necessary adjustments, and keep going on to the next opportunity, the next door, the next level, and whatever else God has for you. It's okay. You can do it. I'm so excited for you! We're almost there! Smile! You're doing this! LIVE!!! #iSpeakLife

❖ *Write it Out* ❖

Think about a time when God showed you something but you ignored it. How did that work out for you?

Day Twenty-Three:
When They Fail You

"Now I know that the Lord saves his anointed; he will answer him
from his holy heaven with the saving might of his right hand.
Some trust in chariots and some in horses, but we trust in the name
of the Lord our God. They collapse and fall, but we rise and stand
upright.

Psalm 20:6-8 (ESV)

~ Today's Declaration ~

There is, there has never been, nor will there ever be ANY failure in
God.

As you know, people will fail you. It's inevitable. Not
everyone is who they say they are. Not everyone can do what they
say they can do. Not everyone can be who they say they can be.
It's not fun finding this out, but it is inevitable.

Having said that, it is important to have a plan in place to be
able to effectively handle and recover from the times of
disappointment we will face when dealing with others. It is
important to make sure that we are prepared. That takes a lot of the
sting out of the situation.

This is the more strategic portion of the devotional. By now, you have a good foundation of knowledge and encouragement. Now it's time to do some planning.

People WILL fail you. I PROMISE you. Just as sure as there are twenty-four hours in a day, someone is going to fail you. You can't let that take you off your course. You can't let that make you give up. You have to have a plan.

A good place to start is to make sure that you are not trusting in people to the same magnitude and degree that you trust in God. You have to always remember that you don't always hit the mark, and no one else will either. You have to KNOW this when dealing with people. ALL of your trust has to be in God.

There is a difference between trusting something and trusting in something. When you sit down, you trust that the chair will hold you. However, your ability to sit down isn't locked and tied up in that particular chair. That chair is not the only chair that can support you. There is always the possibility that the chair will buckle, fall, be wet, etc. That's how we have to be with people. They can be our friends, family, or whatever, and we can really trust that they are going to be there for us when we need them, but not to the point that our lives are drastically altered if they don't meet our expectations. The latter is not healthy at all.

A lot of my suicide attempts came from a misappropriation of trust. I expected people to be so much for me, and when they failed me, I felt like something was wrong with me. I had to realize that just as I'm not perfect, neither are they. As we come to the end of our thirty days together, it is important that you grasp this concept. Do all you can to get it in your head. Trust me. You'll thank me for this.

Today is the day that you use the "Write it Out" to create your action plan. Make it a good one! If you need help, feel free to reach out to me.

I speak courage to you. I decree that God will anchor you in the fact that it is in God that you should and must place all of your trust. You can do it. You're ready. I believe it. We're gonna be just fine when this is all over. Preparation is key! LIVE out loud today knowing that God is right there helping you to "rise and stand upright" just like the scripture says! #iSpeakLife

❋❋ *Write it Out* ❋❋

How have you handled disappointments in the past? How will you handle them from this day forward?

Day Twenty-Four:
Your Day

Scripture:

~ Today's Declaration ~

    I'm proud of you. I'm proud of the progress you've made. This is YOUR day. What scripture(s) will you read today? What's will you declare? What's on your heart?

    Write it out! You already know. #iSpeakLife

Day Twenty-Five:
Getting Your Mind Right

"Do not be conformed to this world, but be transformed by the renewal of your mind, that by testing you may discern what is the will of God, what is good and acceptable and perfect."

Romans 12:2 (ESV)

~ Today's Declaration ~

There is power in the words that I speak and the thoughts that I think, so I will speak and think with intentional precision and clarity.

Mindset is everything. Most of the people who go through the same cycles over and over do so because of their mindset. You can change your location, your job, your car, house, or anything else - if your mindset doesn't change, you will be the exact same person in that new location, on that new job, with that new car, house, and everything else. That's not what God wants for you. That's not what I want for you. That's not what you should want for yourself.

We know that scientifically speaking, our brain is our body's "computer". I like to say that our mindset is our life's "computer". Our mindset dictates so much that happens in our life. When you are negative, you attract negative people. When you are miserable, you attract other miserable people. When you change your mindset and begin to think about success and prosperity, you attract people who can help you get there.

Before you blame anyone else for the lifestyle that you have, check your mindset. Before you blame anyone else for the way you feel, check your mindset. I can almost guarantee you that the two will go hand in hand.

This is our action plan to deal with our mindsets. Are you ready? Look at us! We're on Day 25! Wow!!! Home stretch! Okay - here we go. This is what we're gonna do:

Philippians 4:4-9

"Rejoice in the Lord always; again I will say, rejoice. Let your reasonableness be known to everyone. The Lord is at hand; do not be anxious about anything, but in everything by prayer and supplication with thanksgiving let your requests be made known to God. And the peace of God, which surpasses all understanding, will guard your hearts and your minds in Christ Jesus. Finally, brothers, whatever is true, whatever is honorable, whatever is just, whatever is pure, whatever is lovely, whatever is commendable, if there is any excellence, if there is anything worthy of praise, think about these things. What you have learned and received and heard and seen in me—practice these things, and the God of peace will be with you."

We're gonna do ALL of that. Every day, I want you to set aside time to think on things that are true. Honorable. Just. Pure. Lovely. Commendable. Things that have a spirit of excellence. Things that are worthy of praise. I want you to

INTENTIONALLY think about these things - whatever they are. Watch your life begin to change even more than it already has.

Read God's promises to you. Find motivational quotes to read. Find noteworthy news stories to read. Read about people who are performing random acts of kindness. Read about people who are feeding the hungry and helping the homeless. Read about college graduates. Think about what you want to do in life. Read about someone who is already doing it. Think about the goals you have. Go on YouTube and find someone who is already very successful doing what you want to do. Fill your mind with good things. It works.

We're gonna make it. We're gonna be okay. We are getting stronger and stronger every day. I'm so proud of you!!!

Let's make this a POWERFUL and VICTORIOUS day!!! You can do it! You've already started!!! LIVE! #iSpeakLife

✳✳ *Write it Out* ✳✳

Name five mindsets that you want to get rid of. Name five mindsets that you want to adopt. How will you achieve this?

Na'Kole Watson

Day Twenty-Six:
What If I Told You...?

"Now there were four men who were lepers at the entrance to the gate. And they said to one another, 'Why are we sitting here until we die? If we say, 'Let us enter the city,' the famine is in the city, and we shall die there. And if we sit here, we die also. So now come, let us go over to the camp of the Syrians. If they spare our lives we shall live, and if they kill us we shall but die.' So they arose at twilight to go to the camp of the Syrians. But when they came to the edge of the camp of the Syrians, behold, there was no one there. For the Lord had made the army of the Syrians hear the sound of chariots and of horses, the sound of a great army, so that they said to one another, 'Behold, the king of Israel has hired against us the kings of the Hittites and the kings of Egypt to come against us.' So they fled away in the twilight and abandoned their tents, their horses, and their donkeys, leaving the camp as it was, and fled for their lives. And when these lepers came to the edge of the camp, they went into a tent and ate and drank, and they carried off silver and gold and clothing and went and hid them. Then they came back and entered another tent and carried off things from it and went and hid them."

II Kings 7:3-8 (ESV)

What if I told you that the lepers surely would have died if they sat at the gate? What if I told you that the lepers got to eat and drink and carry off the treasures from the camp ONLY because they made a step? What if I told you that God orchestrated my life to be the way that it was so that I would sit on my couch on this day and write to you so that you could understand that you're not alone in this at all, and that God is with you? What if I told you that you have come further in the last twenty-six days than you have in the last year of your life?

What if I told you that I KNOW within myself that you are much different and in a much better place than you were when you first started this journey? What if I told you that you will do for others what God has used me to do for you? What if I told you that there was a purpose for all of your pain, and that even now, you are beginning to see the beauty in what God was developing in the darkness? What if I told you that God has empowered you to stand in boldness and bring healing to someone else? What if I told you that nothing you went through was in vain? What if I told you that from this moment on, you can do anything you put your mind to do?

What if I told you that despite your flaws, despite your shortcomings, and despite your insecurities, you are loved in a way that surpasses any and every good thing on this earth. What if I told you that God was smiling right now? What if I told you that the grace of God is wrapping itself around you, hugging you, holding you, and strengthening you for the days ahead. What if I told you that many people DIED in what you just came out of? What if I told you that the hand of God is always there protecting you? What if I told you that you are the most amazing creation that God has ever made?

What if I told you that no matter what happens after today, you will ALWAYS be covered, and you will ALWAYS have the ability to go before God's throne and obtain mercy and the strength to keep going. What if I told you that all that has happened over the past twenty-six days of transformation had very little to do with me and everything to do with you? What if I told you that God loves you enough to allow me to go through ALL OF what has happened to me just so that I could get to you? What if I told you that the sky was never the limit and that there are no limits? What would you do if I told you all of that?

I just did.

Now do it. No writing today. Just DOing. Let your life be your declaration today. Feel free to write freely. LIVE. #iSpeakLife

Na'Kole Watson

Day Twenty-Seven:

My Proof

"Am I not free? Am I not an apostle? Have I not seen Jesus our
Lord? Are not you my workmanship in the Lord? If to others I am
not an apostle, at least I am to you, for you are the seal of my
apostleship in the Lord."

1 Corinthians 9:1-2 (ESV)

~ Today's Declaration ~

There is somebody somewhere who is waiting to hear my story.

In 2012, I started digging into suicide prevention research. I
ran across a story of a girl who had died by suicide after being
severely. As I began to put a conference call together to talk about
suicide prevention, I ran across a young lady. She is a minor, so I
won't mention her name. She mentioned on Facebook that she had
attempted suicide the same night that the young lady had. God told
me to reach out to her, and I did. Awkward! I did it, though.

I wrote her a nice note of encouragement, and then I went
on with my life. Three months went by. I was heading to sleep,

and God told me to reach out to her again. I said, "Nah, that's weird. I'm not doing that." I went to sleep.

AS SOON as I got to sleep, I began to cough uncontrollably. I was so irritated. God spoke to me again and told me to reach out to the young lady. Reluctantly, I did. I said what God told me to say. She wrote me back. She told me that she had been sitting there contemplating suicide, and had I not reached out to her, she probably would have gone through with it.

Every time God would tell me to reach out to her, I would. To the glory of God, she has gone from being a drug-addicted teenager who had to go to rehab to someone who has a GED and a job. Not only that, but she is working toward getting her high school diploma just because she wants to have it. Let me tell you something: You are not here by chance. NOTHING that you have gone through is by chance. ALL of it will help someone get out of what they're in. God is amazing.

Last year, my organization did a sock drive for homeless shelters in the area. This young lady sent me a Christmas card with a pair of socks in it, and this is what she said:

"Merry Christmas! Not much is going to be in this envelope, since they're small and I can't fit a lot into them. I'm sending a separate one with the rest. I know it's not a lot, but I hope it helps, even if it just helps one or two people. Happy Holidays!"

This. From someone I've never met in person, and would have never even known had God not told me to get online and do research about suicide prevention, which probably would have never even been a thought if I hadn't attempted so many times. It all works together. Remember that. What you have endured, what you're going through now, and what's up ahead: it ALL works together.

LIVE. You're helping somebody. Trust me. I'm proud of you. If you don't have your proof yet, you will. Just hold on. #iSpeakLife

❋ *Write it Out* ❋

If someone were to write a testimonial about how your life has impacted them, what would you want them to say?

Na'Kole Watson

Day Twenty-Eight:
With All of My Might

"Whatever your hand finds to do, do it with your might; for there is no work or device or knowledge or wisdom in the grave where you are going."

Ecclesiastes 9:10 (NKJV)

~ Today's Declaration ~

I will do better. I will BE better.

Whatever your hands find to do... Do it with all of your might. There is NOTHING you can do from the grave. There's nothing you can do when this life is over. You don't get a do-over. You can't get up out of the casket and walk around and finish up your unfinished business. It doesn't work that way. Never has. You have an allotment of time that you're working with. It's important to get everything accomplished within that timeframe. Don't let your goals, dreams, and visions be buried with you. We have work to do.

If you were supposed to be gone, you would be gone. No matter what you have done, and no matter what you have tried, you are still here. There's a purpose in that. Don't let your pain be in vain. I always tell people: If you don't walk in your purpose, if you give up right here, you will NEVER know what your pain was for. You will NEVER know. Why would you want to sacrifice your whole life to be able to have a mansion and never get to see the mansion? That would be insane... but that's what we do every time we stay in our past and/or our place of comfort or lack. That's not what God has for us.

Writing this book has taken a lot out of me. I have cried. I have felt lonely. I have felt like there was no point in even completing this manuscript. I have had to fight the voice of the enemy in my ear time and time and time again... But here I am... right now... typing with all my might.

I was worried that people wouldn't buy my book. I was worried that those close to me wouldn't support my efforts. I was worried that I was wasting my time. But... You are reading my book. Right now. That one thing makes it worth it. It hasn't manifested yet, because I'm still here writing, but by faith I KNOW that this book will reach you, and I KNOW that you will benefit from it. So... with all my might, I'm writing. I'm tired, I want this to be over, but I am writing. I'm almost there. So are you. Keep going.

You may not be writing a book. You may be speaking. You may be blogging. You may be volunteering at the homeless shelter, opening a soup kitchen, researching, reading, interviewing people, saving money - WHATEVER it is... DO IT... with ALL... of your might. ALL of it. ALL OF IT. Someone is waiting.

Say it with me... You know what I'm about to say. I speak life. To your visions, to your dreams, to your purpose, to those who are waiting to meet you and hear from you... I speak life. #iSpeakLife

❖❖ *Write it Out* ❖❖

Find five scriptures that tell you that you can live a better life. Write them down, and commit them to memory.

Day Twenty-Nine:

Endless Love

"It is he who remembered us in our low estate, for his steadfast love endures forever; and rescued us from our foes, for his steadfast love endures forever; he who gives food to all flesh, for his steadfast love endures forever. Give thanks to the God of heaven, for his steadfast love endures forever."

Psalm 136:23-26 (ESV)

~ Today's Declaration ~

I will ALWAYS be loved by God.

If there is one thing that will always amaze me, it is the love of God. You've got to think about it. There are at least one hundred billion GALAXIES. There are billions and billions of planets. God created ALL of that. There are places in the ocean that have never been touched by any human or any type of manmade apparatus. There are places on this earth that have yet to be discovered. There are species of sea life that we still have yet to discover. There are things about our planet that we have yet to learn. There are species of animals that lived in the past that we are just now discovering. There are things in space that are literally millions of years away... and NONE OF THAT compares to the love that God has for you.

That love is bigger than EVERYTHING. It's deeper. It's wider. It has been around longer. When everything is said and done, and what we know now is no more, that same exact love will be right there. It's a furious love. It's a never-ending love. It's powerful. It transcends time and space. It's bigger than everything you can imagine multiplied by everything you can't imagine. NOTHING compares to it. It's EVERYTHING. Literally.

That love is reaching for you. That love is desiring you. That love is calling out to you. That love forgives you. That love accepts you. That love WANTS you. This is what I want you to do. Say, "God, tell me about Your love." Listen... Write. Write what you hear. Write what you see. Write what you feel. That's your "Write it Out" for today. God loves you. ENDLESSLY. God wants you to have MORE. More of what will help you to succeed. More of what brings you joy. More of what heals you. More of what breaks your chains. MORE. ALL of that is in God. All of it. ALL of it.

Learn to LIVE in that endless love. You can do it. One more day. We're almost there. I'm proud of you. So proud! Live. #iSpeakLife

Day Thirty:

Now.

"On the way to Jerusalem he was passing along between Samaria and Galilee. And as he entered a village, he was met by ten lepers, who stood at a distance and lifted up their voices, saying, 'Jesus, Master, have mercy on us.' When he saw them he said to them, 'Go and show yourselves to the priests.' And as they went they were cleansed. Then one of them, when he saw that he was healed, turned back, praising God with a loud voice; and he fell on his face at Jesus' feet, giving him thanks. Now he was a Samaritan. Then Jesus answered, 'Were not ten cleansed? Where are the nine? Was no one found to return and give praise to God except this foreigner?' And he said to him, 'Rise and go your way; your faith has made you well.'"

Luke 17:11-19 (ESV)

~ Today's Declaration ~

NOW is the time. I am responsible for my life.

YOU DID IT!!!! Today is the last day. You did it. I can't tell you how proud I am of you. I am so so so so proud! I could cry! I am sitting here smiling at the thought of you getting through all of these stories, scriptures, lines on the paper, all of it. I am SO PROUD of you.

Thank you SO MUCH for sticking this out. Thank you SO MUCH for doing the work. I appreciate it, and I know your soul appreciates it. Thank you, thank you, thank you!

Now… Now. Now is the time to move forward. This is it. There's no better time. Now. Right now. Put one foot in front of the other, and keep going. You can always refer back to this book any time you get ready - and as a matter of fact, I encourage you to. I recommend it. You'll be surprised by how much you've grown.

Listen. Jesus went to a village. He saw the lepers. They asked for mercy. He simply told them to go and show themselves to the priests. The Bible says that they were healed AS THEY WENT. They had to make steps. They had to start walking. ALL OF THEM were healed. ALL OF THEM. However, only one turned around, went back to Jesus, and thanked Him. Guess what he was? Yep. A Samaritan. Remember? Yes indeed. A Samaritan. Amazing.

You don't owe me anything. I just ask that you let the way you LIVE be your "thank you". Let your LIFE be your praise to God. YOUR faith made you well. It wasn't my doing. You should feel so good! I have tears of joy in my eyes right now because YOU DID IT! Wow. YOU DID IT! Celebrate!

There's no "Write it Out" today. If you want to write anything, feel free. Just live. That's all. Live. #iSpeakLife

If you struggle or know someone who is struggling with suicidal thoughts, please seek help. The National Suicide Prevention Lifeline is available day and night, and there are plenty of qualified and trained professionals there to help. You can call, you can get someone else to call for you, or you can call for a friend. Just make the call if you need to. Please.

1-800-273-8255 (TALK)

Thanks again for reading my book. I really appreciate it. May God continue to bless you and give you everything your heart desires that is in accordance with God's purpose for your highest good.

I invite and encourage you to check out my website: NOMW.org. You will find out about my nonprofit suicide prevention, anti-bullying, and social advocacy organization, #NotOnMyWatch™. If you ever need anything that my organization provides, please do not ever hesitate to reach out.

Please be sure to go to Amazon and leave a review so that I will know how this book has touched you. If you would like to get in touch with me, you can always call **919-295-2172** or email **connect@nomw.org** and I will gladly get back to you. I appreciate your time and the work you have put in for the betterment of your life. That's awesome.

Always remember that you are never alone.

God bless you.